ALCAZAR
A TO Z INC

THE STORY OF CONRAN RESTAURANTS

TERENCE CONRAN

A LCAZAR
TO Z INC

THE STORY OF CONRAN RESTAURANTS

Photography by Georgia Glynn Smith

conran
OCTOPUS

Alcazar 9

Bibendum 19

Blue Print Café 29

Bluebird 37

Butlers Wharf
Chop House 55

George 100

Miyabi 104

Terminus 112

Guastavino's 117

Mezzo 131

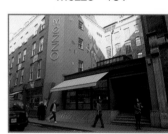

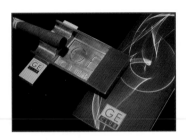

Introduction

THIS IS A BOOK ABOUT THE DESIGN AND STYLE OF OUR RESTAURANTS, BARS, CAFÉS, CLUBS AND DELIS. Although it concentrates on the atmosphere rather than on the food, it does try to give you a taste of what we put on your plate. I believe food always comes first, then the quality and friendliness of the staff, and finally the design of the place. If you can get all three right then you can get that famous and all too often elusive buzz that makes a restaurant a success year after year.

Creating this atmosphere is a complex design exercise because a restaurant is a busy place – even frantic at times in the kitchens – and yet to the customers the whole place must appear as organized, comfortable and relaxing as possible. The reality of a restaurant is that it's a bustling manufactory on one side and a peaceful retailer on the other.

The atmosphere you design depends on many things – including the location, the size of the restaurant, the type of food you plan to serve and, of course, the price you intend to charge. Will it be big and buzzing, or cool, calm and sophisticated? Although we have a reputation for large restaurants, in fact we have only four – Quaglino's, Mezzo, Bluebird and Guastavino's – though on a sunny day when all the terraces are open and the barbecues flaming, Coq d'Argent can appear pretty large and busy, too. Most of our restaurants are medium-sized; Miyabi, the smallest, has just 28 seats. There is no formula for success based on scale, and each type of restaurant appeals to different people, at different times, for different occasions and for different reasons. Curiously, you can be more private in a large restaurant than a small one, sitting by yourself reading a newspaper and watching the world go by.

Of course, like all the restaurant critics, I believe that the ideal would be a small family restaurant run with passion and dedication. When I was young, these family restaurants existed in every town in France and Italy – but sadly this is no longer the case. The hours of work – at least twelve hours a day, six days a week – simply do not comply either with EU edicts or the ambitions of the leisure generation. All the same, even today I'm quite sure that nobody should contemplate starting a restaurant unless they are prepared to work extremely hard and to become immersed in and totally dedicated to their project.

Restaurants are all about detail, and not just the obvious things such as flowers, cutlery and tableware, chairs, tables, and napkins. 'Detail' also encompasses the ergonomic aspects, such as, for example, the design of the waiters' stations that allows the staff to do their jobs easily, or the design of the kitchens, storage areas, preparation space, staff changing rooms and lavatories. The processing and removal of rubbish is not a particularly romantic part of the restaurateur's life, but it is essential to the smooth running of the kitchen and needs detailed consideration and design. In fact, there is a huge amount of careful thought that needs to go into the whole cleaning process; just imagine the quantities of tableware, kitchen equipment and pots and pans that get used day and night. It's a big logistical task to see that the kitchen operates like a well-run workshop because only then will good food emerge from it – hot or chilled, well presented and on time.

Another consideration is the durability of all the equipment we design and specify, not only in the kitchen areas but in the customer side of the restaurant as well. There are few places in this world that get more heavily used and abused than a restaurant. Some customers seem to believe that their space belongs solely to them when they occupy it but unfortunately don't treat the furniture or equipment as they would their own. The cleaners, too, sometimes seem to believe they are in some kind of war zone, in which the restaurant equipment is their deadliest enemy. The designer has to take all this into account and construct objects that are able to withstand the onslaught, can be easily maintained and hopefully over time gain a patina that in itself can be attractive.

Developing our collection of restaurants, starting with Bibendum in 1987, has been one of the most exciting things I have done in my life. Although I would never claim that we started the restaurant revolution in London, we have played quite a major part in it. We have contributed to people's enjoyment of a city that, in the post-war years, had a unenviable reputation for the quality of its restaurants. We now have eating places and food as good as, if not better than, any other city in the world, as well as our own restaurant culture, with customers and critics who are discerning, well informed and appreciative.

The revolution has occurred because new restaurants opened that were enjoyable places to be, where the food was good and the service pleasant. They were an affordable alternative to simply going home to cook after work or a trip to the cinema, theatre or concert hall. They gave people the opportunity to meet their friends and socialize, something that the impersonality of so much of modern life increasingly precludes. The simple truth is that the public didn't know this was something they wanted until it was offered to them – beautifully – on a plate. Now it has become an integral part of city life, and I'm proud that we have been a part of it, and will continue to be as the restaurant, bar, café and club world develops in the future.

Left A view of the restaurant from the bar. The centrepiece of this double-height space is a huge suspended vase, made by Michael Savage. Every two days it is lowered and filled with a fresh display of flowers by Christian Tortu amongst others.
Opposite page:
Left Ground plan of the restaurant; **Right** The entrance doors display Alcazar's distinctive logo – *AZ*.

A/Z

Ever since my stint of washing-up and vegetable peeling in Paris in the mid-fifties, I have longed to open a restaurant there. One day a charming man called Michel Besmond came to see me. He was passionately keen to run a restaurant with our kind of style in Paris, and suggested a property in the rue Mazarine on the Left Bank that might fit the bill.

The space was fantastic but absolutely derelict, and the rent just about affordable. It had originally been the biggest print shop in Europe, but later it had become a rather saucy restaurant-cum-transvestite-cabaret called Alcazar. Underneath all this, in the cellar, was a failed nightclub called Whisky à Gogo, famous as the spiritual home of Jim Morrison.

The massive task of redesign and reconstruction began with plans to open a restaurant and kitchen on the ground floor, with a large bar and private room on the balcony. Nothing is simple when it comes to the design and specification of a large restaurant, especially when it's in an historic building in Paris. We had to get twenty-seven different permissions, and all the latest edicts from Brussels had to be strenuously applied. Certainly we had never before suffered bureaucracy on this scale. When the restaurant eventually opened, we were convinced we were the only totally legal restaurant in France.

The design of the restaurant itself received a lot of press exposure – much of it complimentary. While we kept to some of the principles of the traditional French brasserie, such as the use of easily moveable small tables and banquettes, many ideas, such as the large open kitchens, the double-height space, the light and colour, and the food itself broke with tradition. Obviously we had no intention of trying to become a starred restaurant; our idea was to be buzzy and democratic, reflecting the end of the twentieth century in much the same way that many of the *grandes brasseries* that survive today reflect the end of the

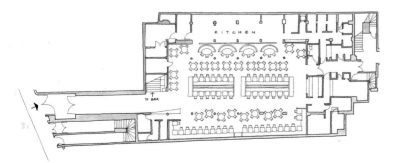

nineteenth. This required a contemporary design, a different approach to food that still connected to the basic brasserie style, and a staff with a modern attitude to service.

When we opened we received some rather stiff reviews from a few of the food critics – a bit surprising as both the manager, Michel Besmond, and the chef (recruited from Taillvent, the most famous of all three-star establishments in Paris) are French. However, Alcazar has become more and more successful and seems to have now found a place in the minds, hearts and stomachs of Parisians.

It's a lovely, happy place, filled with light and humour, good food,

music and drink. In fact, it has become *'le hot-spot de Paris'*.

The mezzonine bar: from informal dining to late-night dancing

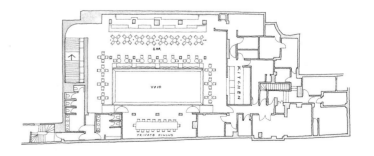

In the evening, as the light gradually dims to a romantic glow, the mezzonine bar transforms itself from an elegant space to have lunch or an early dinner to a very busy and energetic place to drink and dance the night away. Alcazar's late-night music has become famous, with a CD compilation of its sounds selling all over Paris and London. Also on the mezzonine is a large, well-insulated private room, much used by the fashion press for parties and presentations.
Left Plan of the mezzonine bar.

Details inspired by Alcazar's past glories

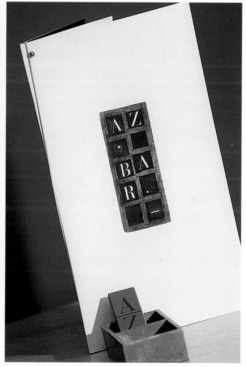

Opposite page: **Above** The staircase from the reception to the mezzanine bar is decorated with a vibrant wall painting by Javaid Alvi as well as with bowls of flowers; **Below** The passage leading from the front door displays photographs and books, a reflection of the fact that the restaurant is situated at the heart of the Parisian publishing quarter. **This page: Top left** Pinch pots for salt and cracked pepper can also be used as ashtrays. **Top right** A reproduction of the original Alcazar publicity from the 1960s, with endorsements from some of France's greatest cultural icons. **Bottom left** Wine glasses with our AZ symbol. **Bottom right** The graphics for Alcazar are inspired by the printing-blocks that would have been used when the space functioned as a printworks.

Recipes from Alcazar

CHEF: Guillaume Lutard MANAGER: Michel Besmond

Tartare de Dorade

STARTER Serves 4

The fish must be absolutely fresh since it is
being served raw. This makes a delicate and
fresh-tasting summery first course.

4 sea bream fillets, skin and pin-bones removed	1 shallot, peeled and finely chopped
1 tbsp mayonnaise	4 medium-sized oysters
juice of 1 lime	1 tbsp extra-virgin olive oil
1 tbsp chives, chopped	salt and pepper
	1 lime, to serve

Chop the fish into very small pieces and place in
a bowl with the mayonnaise, lime juice, chives
and shallot. Open the oysters, add the liquid to
the bowl and discard the shells. Chop the
oysters finely and add to the mixture with all the
liquid from the chopping board. Add the olive oil
and season to taste with salt and pepper.

Mound in the centre of 4 cold plates and
serve with a quarter of lime on each, offering
warm toast at the table.

Gambas Sautées aux Epices

MAIN Serves 4

sauce:	2 leeks, julienne
1 green pepper	1 red pepper, julienne
½ tsp ginger powder	2 courgettes, julienne
1 tsp curry powder	30 g preserved ginger
½ tsp turmeric	1 kg tiger prawns, shelled
¼ tsp cinnamon	handful coriander leaves, chopped
200 ml single cream	
2 carrots, peeled and julienne	75 ml light olive oil
	salt and pepper

Preheat the oven to 100 °C.

Destalk and deseed the pepper. Cut into small
pieces, mix with the spices and put in an
ovenproof dish. Bake for 1 hour. Transfer to a
food processor, add the cream and blitz to a
purée. Pour into a saucepan and keep warm
over a low heat.

Heat 3 tbsp of the oil in a wok over a medium
to high heat, add the vegetables and ginger, and
stir-fry for 2–3 minutes. Season to taste and
remove from the heat.

In another pan, heat the remaining oil until
smoking hot and fry the prawns for 1 minute on
each side.

Mix the spiced vegetables with the prawns.

To serve, divide between 4 warmed plates,
pouring the sauce around. Garnish with the
coriander and serve immediately.

Poached Pears, Chocolate Sauce and Cinnamon Ice Cream

DESSERT Serves 4

Poaching demands slightly under-ripe pears;
too ripe and they will fall apart. The cinnamon
ice cream needs to be churned in a machine.

4 slightly under-ripe pears	300 ml whipping cream
300 g sugar	chocolate sauce:
1 vanilla pod	500 g dark chocolate
cinnamon ice cream:	150 g glucose
500 ml full-fat milk	600 g milk
6 cinnamon sticks	whipped cream:
9 egg yolks	600 ml whipping cream
225 g caster sugar	60 g icing sugar
1 tsp ground cinnamon	3 drops vanilla essence

Make the ice cream: bring water to a simmer in
a saucepan over which you can place a bowl in
which to cook the custard.

Put the milk and cinnamon sticks in a pan and
bring to the boil slowly over a low heat.

Whisk the egg yolks, sugar and cinnamon
together in a metal or glass bowl until pale.
Pour the scalded milk into this mixture, whisking
until incorporated.

Place the bowl over the simmering water and
stir continuously with a wooden spoon until you
have a custard thick enough to coat the back of
the spoon. Add the ground cinnamon, pass
through a sieve into a bowl and leave to cool to
room temperature.

Whip the cream just to the point where it
starts to thicken, then fold it into the custard.
Pour and scrape into the ice-cream maker and
churn until just set. Transfer to a plastic box with
a lid and freeze overnight.

Peel the pears, leaving the stems on. Put in a
pan with the sugar and vanilla pod and 1 litre of
water. Bring to the boil, turn down the heat to a
simmer and put a plate or a small lid on top to
keep them beneath the surface. Poach gently
for 30 minutes, or until just cooked. Remove
from the heat and leave the pears to cool in
the liquid.

Make the chocolate sauce: break the
chocolate into pieces and put in a bowl over
very hot but not boiling water. Put the milk in a
pan with the glucose and bring to the boil. Pour
over the chocolate and whisk together to mix
completely. Keep warm over the water.

Whip the cream with the vanilla until thick and
add the icing sugar.

To serve, put a scoop of ice cream in the
centre of a plate and sit a pear on top. Pour
over the warm chocolate sauce and serve with
the cream.

Offering fine contemporary French cooking, but with some British dishes too, Alcazar is fashionable and beautiful and very *Parisien*.

Left The light that streams through the roof and the stained-glass windows at Bibendum is all part of the enjoyment of this beautiful space. The stained glass in the main restaurant depicts Monsieur Bibendum happily drinking broken glass, sharp flints and nails, as he extols '*Nunc est bibendum*' – 'Now is the time to drink!'.
Opposite page:
Right Monsieur Bibendum with his signature cigar – one of a series of stunning stained-glass windows at the Michelin Building.
Left The first-floor plan of the restaurant.

BIBENDUM

After Habitat opened in a rather dreary building on the Fulham Road in May 1964, I would often look across the road at the marvellous Michelin Building, dreaming about how I could transform it into a wonderful shop and, of course, a first-class restaurant.

I wrote endless letters to the Michelin headquarters in Clermont-Ferrand, asking them what they intended to do with the building, since it appeared, so I pointed out, to be practically unused. One day in 1985, I heard that the company had finally decided to sell it. I rushed to see their managing director and impressed him with my determination to restore this wonderful quirky building to its former glory. I promised to repair all the original features, including the stained-glass windows, the Bibendum-like light fittings on the roof and the damaged faience tiling on the façade. Michelin, I said, would be proud of the old building when it was finished. My enthusiasm won the day, and eventually the company agreed to sell the building to Paul Hamlyn and me for conversion into offices for Paul's publishing company and a huge Conran Shop, as well as a restaurant and oyster bar.

The building had been designed in 1910 as a tyre warehouse, with a bay at the front for weighing cars and fitting tyres. Designed by Michelin engineers, it was the first reinforced-concrete building in the UK. With its change of use, major structural alterations had to be made to make it suitable for its new role. Two floors had to be added, mainly to take plant and air-conditioning equipment. And all this had to be done without changing the appearance of this remarkable building.

For obvious reasons, I was very keen to use the name Bibendum for the restaurant. Apart from anything else, the name was emblazoned across the listed ceramic façade, where Monsieur Bibendum – the original 'Michelin Man' – was also disporting himself in a series of brilliant stained-glass windows. Michelin eventually gave me dispensation, and so we designed the restaurant – including the chairs, tables, china and glassware – to reflect his charming, curvy ebullient form, though not to the extent that the place looked like a theme park. We restored many of the original mosaics and plaques of motoring exploits and designed new interior details that echoed them.

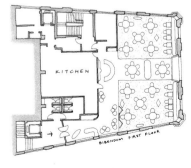

BIBENDUM FIRST FLOOR

We used the ground floor and the lobby as an oyster bar, for which the tyre bay served as the kitchen. We also installed a Citroën 2CV as a van for seafood sales and a Citroën market van for flower sales. (To these, we have recently added a small coffee bar.) These activities, which reflect the Michelin heritage, make a wonderfully busy entrance to the whole building. Upstairs is a serious restaurant with about eighty seats, serving sophisticated brasserie food.

Left The jovial spirit of Monsieur Bibendum presides over the diners in the main restaurant. **Above** The reception desk with a coat-hanger-cum-light. **Opposite page: Main picture** The restaurant is decorated with Michelin posters and 'Mich' cartoons of some of the famous people involved with the automobile world circa 1910. Note, too, the details of the chair and table legs; **Bottom, left to right** Skylights flood the restaurant with natural light; As in all our restaurants, great attention is paid to the design and comfort of our lavatories and bathrooms; China, glass and menus all proudly bear the Bibendum symbol.

The Michelin Man surveys his domain

MARCEL RENAULT

...NNE
1902

Monsieur Bibendum and the world's best company

BIBENDUM COFFEE BAR
TAKE·AWAY PRICES

Espresso	1·10
Cappucino	1·40
Café latte	1·40
Double espresso	1·60
Tall latte	1·80
Tall Cappucin	1·80
Tea, tisane	1·10

Croissant 1·25, Lemon and
mascarpone danish 3·00,
Citronnier 2·0.

his various manifestations throughout the decades. He was recently voted symbol. His charm, image and style are a great inspiration to us.

Bibendum oyster bar and 'fish market' crustacea van

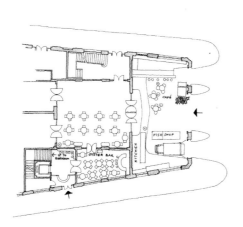

Opposite page: Main picture The oyster bar on the ground floor preserves much of the atmosphere of the original building, with new additions such as the glass doors and screens; **Top left** One of the marvels of the old Michelin Building was the beautiful original mosaic floor of the entrance hall; **Bottom left** The friendly, curvy chairs and chunky metal table pedestals are another homage to Monsieur Bibendum. **This page: Above, left** As well as recalling its former life as a Michelin garage, the tiny oyster bar evokes the polished horseshoe cafés of Paris. A large handsome mirror reflects back the glittering glass-laden bar; **Above, right** The old tyre bay at the front of the building is now used to sell fish and crustacea, prepare food for the oyster bar, and sell flowers, as well as incorporating a small coffee bar. It's also the entrance to the Conran Shop and the offices; **Left** Plan of the ground floor.

Arguably London's most exquisite dining-room, Bibendum continues to serve some of the finest food in the most luxurious of surroundings with good taste, simplicity and style.

Recipes from Bibendum

CHEF: Matthew Harris MANAGING DIRECTOR: Graham Williams

Thai Crab Salad
STARTER Serves 4

If you don't like the idea of cooking a live crab, your fishmonger will be happy to do it for you.

2 large cock crabs or 4 smaller ones	200 ml water
2 hot red chillies, de-seeded and finely chopped	juice of 2 large limes
	2 tsp caster sugar
	bunch of mint, roughly chopped
2 cloves garlic, chopped	bunch of coriander, roughly chopped
50 ml Thai fish sauce	

Put the crab on its back and twist off the claws and legs. Crack the claws open with the back of a heavy knife. A gentle but firm pull will bring away not only the claw meat but also the tip concealed inside the pincer. Repeat with the remaining claw segments then deal with the legs. These have a much softer shell.

Give the tail flap a knock to loosen it before using a knife or screwdriver to lever out the underside panel to which the legs were attached. As you lift it up, it will pull away the bony central section. Reserve. This contains most of the white meat. Behind the mouth you will find the stomach sac and bits. Throw these away, then use a small spoon to scrape out the brown flesh from the outer sections of the shell. Remove and discard the translucent gills ('dead men's fingers') that are curled over the bony central section. Cut down and through this section in a V to give you 4 accessible planes, using a thin skewer to extract all the meat concealed in the little pockets and channels. Turn it the other way up and scrape out the remaining white flesh from the leg sockets.

You now have the prime white and red claw meat, ivory shell meat and brown meat (including the liver) from the shell extremities. You only use white crab meat in this dish. Use the brown meat in something else, for example a soup or a risotto.

Mix the chillies, garlic, fish sauce, lime juice and sugar with 200 ml water. Stir in the herbs.

Divide the crab between 4 cold plates and spoon the dressing around the edge.

Grilled Veal Chop with Anchovy and Rosemary Butter
MAIN Serves 4

A chop is the only cut of veal other than the rear leg that is tender enough to be cooked using dry heat, for example pan-frying or grilling. It should never be overcooked, nor should it be rare. Medium – that is, pink in the middle but with no discernible blood traces – is what you should aim for.

4 x 2.5–3 cm thick veal chops	3 cloves garlic, peeled and finely chopped
1 tbsp olive oil	
salt and pepper	2 bunches of rosemary, picked and chopped
anchovy and rosemary butter:	
Makes 8–10 portions	salt and pepper
250 g unsalted butter	
20 best-quality fillets of salted anchovies in olive oil	

Leave the butter to soften at room temperature in a bowl. Chop the anchovies. Season with lots of pepper, and a touch of salt, before mixing all the ingredients together thoroughly. Mound the butter in a line on a sheet of tinfoil and roll the foil around it, twisting the ends to seal. Refrigerate until needed. If you are not going to use it all, the butter left over will keep in a freezer for a month without deteriorating.

Preheat a ridged grill pan or barbecue to medium hot. Brush the chops with olive oil and season generously with salt and pepper.

A 2.5 to 3-cm-thick chop will cook to medium rare in about 8 minutes. Lay on a ridged grill pan or barbecue preheated to medium hot at an angle of 45 degrees to the ridges or bars. Do not push it around. Cook for 5 minutes and then turn, giving it a further 3–4 minutes. Remove and rest in a warm place for 5 minutes, by which time the moisture in the meat will have redistributed itself from the surface to the middle, leaving the meat a uniform rose pink.

Serve on warm plates with a slice of the rosemary butter, a wedge of lemon and a simple green salad.

Cinnamon Custard Tart
DESSERT Serves 10

1 x 30-cm shortcrust pastry case, baked blind	4 cinnamon sticks
	18 egg yolks
1250 ml double cream	200 g caster sugar
	powdered cinnamon

In a heavy-based saucepan, bring the cream and cinnamon sticks to the boil. Remove from the heat and leave to infuse for at least an hour.

Preheat the oven to 100 °C.

In a bowl, beat together the yolks and sugar until pale and creamy. Reheat the cinnamon cream and pour it through a sieve over the egg yolks, mixing well. Pour this custard into the pastry case and cook at 100 °C for about 40 minutes, until just set.

Remove from the oven and dust with powdered cinnamon. Leave to cool. Serve at room temperature.

Above A reflected view down the length of the restaurant typifies Blue Print's ethos: good, simple design. On the shelf and around the columns are samples of chef Jeremy Lee's excellent preserved fruit and vegetables. **Opposite page** Plan of the Blue Print Café.

BLUE PRINT CAFÉ

An 'ace caff with quite a good museum attached' was how the Saatchi advertising campaign relaunched the V&A. The truth of the matter was that the café was only slightly more focused than the museum, but Roy Strong, the V&A's director at the time, knew the strength of spin.

Blue Print is the extremely well-focused café/restaurant at London's ace Design Museum at Butlers Wharf. While the restaurant is run entirely separately from the museum, the two institutions complement each other very well. Both extol the virtues of form following function and the intelligent manipulation of quality raw materials to produce eye-catching, pleasurable results.

Blue Print opened in 1991, shortly after the museum. Situated on the first floor, it boasts a large glazed balcony with spectacular views up and down the Thames. The design is very simple. The oak floors, white walls and white ceiling are perfectly matched by the Thonet Bentwood furniture, vibrant blue banquettes and red table tops. The only decorations are photographs of designers and architects from the covers of *Blueprint* magazine in its heyday.

The current chef, Jeremy Lee, has a passion for fresh ingredients, simply prepared, and works with many smallholders, fishermen and farmers to secure his supplies. His food reflects the Mediterranean to the Middle East, especially Morocco, Algeria and Turkey. Blue Print was the first of our restaurants at Butlers Wharf and is part of what we call the Gastrodrome.

When I developed Butlers Wharf, I was clearly told by all the knowledgeable and highly paid property agents that a restaurant would never be a success on the South Bank because the City would never cross the Thames for lunch or dinner. We therefore opened Blue Print with some trepidation, although personally I was convinced that its spectacular setting and beautiful design would make the deviation seem worthwhile.

After a hesitant start and a change of chef and manager, we proved the agents wrong and Blue Print has continued to be successful for the last ten years. Indeed, the whole Butlers Wharf complex, with its eight or so restaurants and bars, has proved to be one of the most sought-after restaurant destinations in London. So much for professional advice!

One of the interesting things that Blue Print has demonstrated is that if a restaurant is good enough then it can afford to be off-pitch and that this itself can be a great catalyst for further development. Once a totally derelict part of London, Butlers Wharf is now a thriving, dynamic place, densely packed with new apartments and businesses. Blue Print and the other cafés, bars and restaurants that have followed are responsible for much of this success.

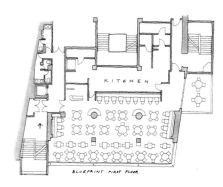

BLUEPRINT FIRST FLOOR

Good design, great food and wonderful views across the river

Above, left to right: Blue Print is on the first floor of London's highly regarded Design Museum. Views over the river encompass the Tower of London, Tower Bridge, Canary Wharf, and, outside the museum, a bronze by Sir Eduardo Paolozzi; Signed photographs of contemporary designers line one wall; Simplicity and style are the mark of Blue Print design: Le Corbusier bentwood chairs, red plastic table tops and bright-blue banquettes. **Below:** Simple, fresh ingredients include a selection of finely crafted breads. **Opposite page: Main picture** The view from the balcony towards Tower Bridge; **Far right, above and below** Blue Print's bold simplicity is carried through into its graphics, even down to the matchboxes. **Following pages:** Fresh ingredients from small producers are integral to Blue Print's food.

An inventive, Mediterranean-inspired menu and simple presentation make the Blue Print Café as much of an attraction as the Design Museum.

Recipes from Blue Print Café

CHEF: Jeremy Lee MANAGER: Richard Hamblin

Moules Marinière
STARTER Serves 4

Made simply, without unnecessary additions and using the best and freshest mussels, this time-honoured classic remains sublime.

2 kg mussels	small handful of
4 small onions,	flat-leaf parsley
peeled and finely	115 g unsalted butter
chopped	salt and pepper
120 ml dry white	
wine	

Remove the beards and set the mussels to rinse under running cold water for 20–30 minutes to get rid of any grit. Don't leave any longer or the flavour will be reduced.

Put the onion in a pan together with the white wine. Place a lid upon the pot and set over a high heat.

Set a colander over a bowl beside the cooker. Add the mussels to the pan and cook with the lid on, shaking regularly. When all the shells have sprung open, tip the mussels into the colander. Return the pot to the stove and decant the cooking liquor from the mussels back into the pot, leaving behind a little that will in all certainty contain grit. Bring the liquid to the boil and chop the parsley not too fine, and add the butter. Whisk well together. Place the mussels in 4 large warmed bowls and pour over the sauce.

Serve with bread and a fine bottle of white Burgundy, putting an empty bowl on the table for the shells.

Roast Grey-leg Partridge
MAIN Serves 4

The grey-leg, or feral, partridge of northern Europe is considered superior to the red-leg partridge of Spain and the South. Though not as large as a red-leg, it has a finer flavour. Typically a young dressed bird will weigh about 350 g and is best simply roasted and served with the classic accompaniments of redcurrant jelly and watercress.

4 grey-leg partridges	redcurrant jelly
100 g unsalted butter	4 bunches
4 thin slices white	watercress
bread cut in	
rounds	

Preheat the oven to 230 °C.

Remove the birds from the refrigerator and leave to come to room temperature before cooking. Cover them with butter and evenly salt and pepper them. Set them not touching in a roasting pan and place in the hot oven.

The birds will take about 18 minutes to roast, and should be basted every 5 minutes or so. The difficulty is getting the legs fully cooked because when they are, the breasts will be overdone and dry. After 18 minutes the birds will be a pale golden colour.

Remove from the oven and set to one side to rest for 10 minutes, though nowhere too warm. During this period, cooking is completed and juices brought to the surface in the oven will be redistributed, delivering a moist result, the legs still pink around the bone.

While the birds rest, fry the bread discs in a little butter until crisp and golden. Transfer them to the roasting pan and allow them to soak up the juices. Put these croutons on warmed plates, placing the birds on top. Serve with watercress on one side of the bird and a dish of redcurrant jelly in a separate bowl. To enhance this dish of perfect simplicity, you need serve nothing else aside from a good Burgundy.

Pears in Vin Santo
DESSERT Serves 4

Should Vin Santo prove too rare and expensive, then use a good Marsala instead. As they are best served barely warm, cook the pears just before dinner.

4 William pears	scrap of bay leaf
2 tbsp caster sugar	115 g mascarpone or
150 ml Vin Santo	Jersey cream
1 vanilla pod	

Heat the oven to 180 °C.

Split the pears straight through the core, cutting through the stalk. Remove the core with a melon baller along with any fibrous matter attached, if possible without removing the stalk.

Put the sugar into a pan over a medium heat and leave to caramelize. Working quickly and carefully, place the pear halves cut-side down in the caramel, and pour over the Vin Santo. Stand back as the sugar may spit. Drop in the vanilla pod, whole, and the bay leaf. Put the pan in the oven and cook for 15–20 minutes, depending on their size. They are done when the pears offer little resistance to the touch. Remove the pan from the oven and spoon some of the syrup over the pears.

Serve with a spoonful of mascarpone or Jersey cream with the syrup poured over.

Above A busy night in the Bluebird restaurant. The food is classically simple, using the very best-quality seasonal ingredients. **Opposite page: Right** First-floor plan of the restaurant; **Far right** A wine label commemorates the achievements of the great Malcolm Campbell.

BLUEBIRD

In the mid-fifties I had a tiny restaurant at the bottom end of the King's Road called Orrery (since reborn, on a rather grander scale and with a rather different menu, in Marylebone). It was almost opposite the Bluebird Garage, then used for ambulances. The garage had been built in the late twenties and had connections to that glamorous hero of motor speed, Malcolm Campbell, who spent the pre-war years breaking records in his wonderful Bluebird cars. I loved the place and felt increasingly sad as it deteriorated further and further, ending up a really sleazy, run-down market.

In 1994 we were approached by agents representing ex-Dire Straits frontman Mark Knopfler. Mark had bought the derelict property and was looking around for someone who could restore something of its old glory. He had seen what we had done with the Michelin garage and believed that we could revitalise another famous Chelsea garage. Of course, we leapt at the chance and started to discuss how we might use the vast 50,000 square feet of space, spread over two floors and basement. A particular worry was the forecourt with its grimy, redundant petrol pumps.

After considerable discussion, we decided that it could become a giant gastrodrome, encompassing a food market, a café, a large restaurant, a dining club, bars and an outdoor plant and flower market, as well as a shop selling table-top and cooking equipment. We also included a huge preparation kitchen and bakery in the basement (to which we've recently added Bluebird 2 You for outside parties). We would keep the Bluebird name and emphasize the Campbell connection, especially in the club.

During the planning the initial focus was on how the derelict structure could be refurbished. A new extra-strong roof had to be constructed to take the huge amount of equipment necessary for the heating, cooling and cooking extraction of the vast spaces beneath, which included four separate kitchens. Eventually all the pieces jigsawed together and the detailed design started. We decided that the forecourt would be granite cobblestones, and we built a beautiful glass-covered market canopy with flames rising from it at night. We decided how the café could spill out onto this area on sunny days.

The market is very simple with separate, shop-like areas for meat, fish, cheese, bread and pâtisserie (baked in our own kitchens), coffee,

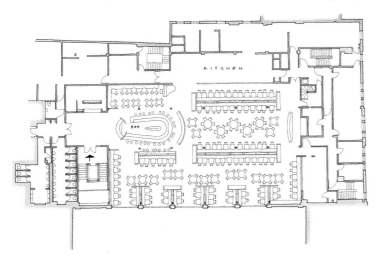

A view of the Bluebird gastrodrome, with its bustling outside market and café. The main restaurant is on the first floor, above the indoor food market.

wine, fruit and vegetables, charcuterie and, of course, a deli. Everyday groceries are displayed on simple plywood shelving that runs down the centre.

The restaurant is reached by a lift and staircase and retains its industrial feel. The old garage riveted-steel roof has been refurbished and repainted and sports a giant floating kite-like sculpture by Richard Smith. The kitchen is open to the restaurant and dominated by a large wood-fired oven. Much of the cooking is inspired by the burning wood and is simple and generous, with some occasional Asian elements. A huge crustacea counter and

display is the focal point of this dramatic space. A small private room was constructed in the eaves to look down on the huge buzzing restaurant below.

The Bluebird Club has its own entrance and comfortable bar on the ground floor. Upstairs is a wonderful glass-roofed dining room, with simple, comfortable furniture. The walls are covered with pictures, mementos and photographs of Malcolm Campbell's record-breaking exploits and his cars. The graphics for the club are 301.129, Campbell's final world speed record in 1931.

Bluebird was originally a beautiful 1920s garage where Malcolm Campbell is said to have assembled his world speed record cars – the Bluebirds.

At Bluebird speed has been exchanged for relaxation

Left An open market with a cobbled pavement now replaces the greasy tarmac and petrol pumps of the old garage. **Below, far left** Plan of the café. **Below, left** In summer, the courtyard becomes a very popular extension to the café, with an open barbecue. **Below** The glazed canopy over the outdoor market protects the produce from rain and shine. **Below, right** In the food market is a fresh juice bar. **Below, far right** Café food is simple and delicious and relies on the quality of our own baked breads. **Right** The interior of the café – simple furniture for simple food and drink.

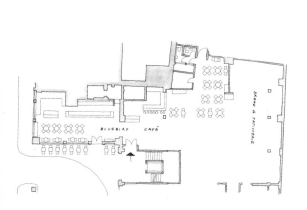

The Bluebird food market: small, specialist shops for food lovers

The Bluebird Restaurant

Opposite page: **Far left, top to bottom** The coat check with a Bibendum chair by Eileen Grey; The lavatories are well designed and spacious. **Main picture** The large bar is aptly reminiscent of the exhaust pipes of a large, powerful racing car. **This page: Left, top to bottom** Details matter – the wine cooler with feet like a bird, cantilever chairs, and graphics for menus, wine lists, bags, bills and so on, all incorporating the Bluebird logo; **Right** A view of the restaurant from the private room in the eaves: Dick Smith's kite sculpture soars above the bustle below; **Below, right** The magnificent crustacea bar at one end of the restaurant is a glistening, mouth-watering focal point. **Following pages:** Food preparation and bakery located in the basement kitchen.

Recipes from Bluebird Restaurant

CHEF: Blair Smethurst GENERAL MANAGER: Henry Chebaane

Eggs Benedict

STARTER Serves 4

4 very fresh eggs
1 tbsp wine vinegar
4 slices ham
2 English muffins
1 tsp paprika

hollandaise:
4 egg yolks
125 g unsalted
  butter, diced
3 tbsp lemon juice
salt and pepper

You will need 2 pans of water, one to poach the eggs and the other for the bottom half of a double boiler; the base of the bowl you use for making the hollandaise should sit just above the water without touching it. For the poaching, use a wide shallow pan of lightly salted water. Add the vinegar to this and bring to the boil. The water should bubble, but not too hard.

Bring the second pan to a simmer. Put the egg yolks in a bowl over the water and whisk in the butter a few pieces at a time, whisking continuously until the butter melts. When it is incorporated, remove the bowl and continue whisking off the heat for 1–2 minutes. If the sauce splits at any point, immediately beat in a tablespoon of boiling water.

A teaspoon at a time, add the lemon juice, whisking until fully incorporated. Season with salt and pepper and replace the bowl over the water, whisking continuously until it is as thick as mayonnaise. This should take 3–5 minutes. At this point, remove the bowl from the heat.

Break the eggs into a saucer and slide into the simmering vinegared water. Poach for 2–3 minutes, then remove with a slotted spoon and trim the ragged edges with scissors.

To serve, split two English muffins and toast the flat side only, buttering each half. Put a slice of ham on top, then sit an egg on the ham and spoon the hollandaise over the eggs. Sprinkle with a little paprika and serve at once.

Fish Cakes with Parsley Panada

MAIN Serves 4

500 g coley, haddock
  fillet (any white fish
  will do), pin-boned
450 ml full-fat milk
1 tbsp dry sherry
1 bay leaf
3 spring onions,
  thinly sliced
45 g unsalted butter
45 g flour
nutmeg
salt and pepper

3 tbsp flat-leaf
  parsley, chopped
  finely
450 g peeled floury
  potatoes, boiled
  and mashed dry
150 g fine dry
  breadcrumbs
2–3 eggs, beaten
1 leafy lemon,
  quartered
  lengthways, to
  serve

To make the breadcrumbs, dry slices of fresh white bread in a low oven until dry enough to shatter. Blitz in a food processor.

Remove the skin from the fish and cut into chunks. Bring the milk and sherry to the boil with the bay leaf and skin. Lower the heat and simmer for 15 minutes. Discard the skin and bay leaf, stir in the fish and cook until just opaque. Drain, reserving the milk and the fish separately.

In a heavy-based pan, sweat the onion in the butter until transparent. Make a roux by adding the flour. Whisk in the milk, then add about ¼ nutmeg, grated, and season with salt and pepper. Cook, stirring frequently, over the lowest heat for about 10–12 minutes. Beat in the parsley and reserve. This is a panada.

Mix the panada with the mashed potatoes. Flake the fish and chop. Fold into the mixture. Spread on a Swiss-roll tin. When cool, refrigerate for at least six hours. Portion in 85-g amounts. Roll into balls on a lightly floured surface. Whisk the eggs. Dip the balls one at a time in the beaten eggs then roll in the crumbs. Then *either* preheat a deep fryer to 190 °C and

fry the balls in batches until golden brown – about 3–4 minutes. Drain on kitchen paper before serving with lemon quarters. *Or* shallow fry over a low-to-medium heat in a mixture of olive oil and unsalted butter, turning once. Drain and serve as before.

Chocolate and Pear Tart

DESSERT Serves 8

6 pears
1 lemon
1 orange
225 g caster sugar
1 cinnamon stick
575 ml white wine
575 ml water
**chocolate
frangipane:**
115 g butter
225 g dark chocolate

115 g caster sugar
3 eggs
115 g ground
  almonds
30 g plain flour
1 tbsp flaked
  almonds
1 x 25-cm blind-
  baked sweet
  pastry shell

Peel the pears, place in a saucepan with all the other poaching ingredients and bring to the boil. Lower the heat and poach until not quite soft. Remove from the heat and leave to cool.

Preheat oven to 150 °C.

Allow the butter to soften to room temperature. Melt the chocolate in a bowl over hot water. Beat the butter and sugar until white and creamy, then add the eggs, beating them in a little at a time. Add the ground almonds and flour. Beat in chocolate. Spoon half the frangipane into the pastry shell, arrange the pears, then spoon the rest of the frangipane on top, smoothing the surface. Sprinkle with flaked almonds and bake for 1 hour.

Serve warm or at room temperature on its own or with a spoonful of crème fraîche or clotted cream.

Bluebird serves simple yet delicious food made from the finest seasonal ingredients in a huge airy dining-room.

Bluebird Club and Bar

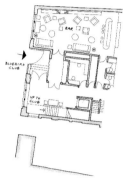

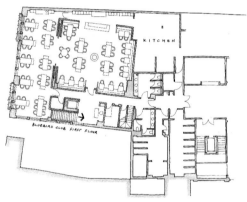

Left The Bluebird Club's comfortable bar on the ground floor has mementoes of Campbell's remarkable achievements, which are also remembered in specially commissioned pictures by Jack Vettriano. Above Floor plans of the club. Opposite page: Main picture Carpets carry the club symbol, 301.129 – Campbell's final speed record; Far right, top The decoration of the mirrors in the club's luxurious bathrooms and lavatories echo the racing-car theme. Far right, bottom The entrance hall features models of some of the Bluebird cars.

The club dining-room enjoys natural light from its elevated glass roof, a room dedicated to the pleasures of the table. Everything suggests comfort from the well-spaced tables to the fine green leather chairs. One wall is given over to wine racks containing the world's finest wines. Other walls are decorated with a fascinating collection of Bluebird memorabilia. The club includes a large private dining room and an elegant cocktail bar.

Recipes from Bluebird Club

CHEF: Iain Loynes MANAGER: Hervé Graciet

Pea Velouté with Scottish Girolles

STARTER Serves 4

This soup is best made when Scottish girolles are in season, but it is also very good with any fresh wild mushroom. It can be served either hot or chilled.

100 g mixed diced vegetables (excluding carrots)	50 g butter
	100 g girolles
	30 g butter
500 ml chicken stock	8 chives
100 ml double cream	4 tbsp whipped
100 g fresh peas	cream
100 g frozen peas	

Over a low heat, sweat the diced vegetables in butter until translucent, then add the chicken stock and cook for 10 minutes. Add the double cream, all the peas, and cook for a further 7–8 minutes. Add salt to taste. Pour into a blender or food processor and blitz for 2–3 minutes until very smooth. If the mixture is too thick, add a small amount of water.

Sauté the girolles in a little butter, then drain on kitchen paper. Place the girolles in warmed serving bowls, pour on the soup and serve garnished with finely chopped chives and some lightly whipped cream.

Roast Poulet de Bresse, Mashed Potatoes, Ceps and Jus Gras

MAIN Serves 4

Bresse chickens are superior birds that have the equivalent of an *appellation contrôlée* definition. No chicken can be called a *poulet de Bresse* unless it has been raised following strictly defined feeding and open-air access regimes. Unsurprisingly, they are expensive but have a superb flavour and texture.

1 or 2 *poulets de Bresse*, depending on the size of bird	30 g unsalted butter
	salt
3 tbsp olive oil	**mashed potato:**
100 ml dry white wine	1 kg floury potatoes, peeled
200 ml chicken stock	60 g butter
100g ceps, cleaned with a damp cloth	3 tbsp double cream
	salt and pepper

Preheat the oven to 200 °C.

Season the bird(s) with sea salt, inside and out, and sprinkle with a small amount of olive oil. Heat 2 tbsp olive oil in a roasting tin over a medium heat and seal the bird until golden brown on all sides.

Roast, breast side up and basting frequently, until cooked – about 45 minutes. Once cooked, leave the bird to rest in a very warm place for 10 minutes.

Cut the potatoes into uniform chunks then boil in lots of lightly salted water.

Drain them through a colander and return to the pan. Shake over a low heat to evaporate all moisture. Mash them dry thoroughly before beating in first the butter and then the cream. The amounts used really depend on how creamy you like your mash. Season to taste with salt and pepper.

Fry the ceps in a little butter, then drain on kitchen paper.

Make the sauce. Put the roasting tin over a medium heat and add the wine. Bring to the boil, scraping vigorously with a wooden spoon to incorporate all the little pieces that have stuck to the tin. Add the chicken stock and reduce to a sauce consistency. Pass through a sieve.

Carve the chicken, cutting off the legs and then cutting through the joint to divide into drumsticks and thighs. Cut the breasts off whole before cutting across on the bias into 4–5 slices.

Spoon some mashed potatoes in the middle of 4 warmed plates, sprinkle over the ceps and place on the carved chicken pieces. Finish with the sauce, and sprinkle with parsley to serve.

Prunes with Vanilla Ice Cream

DESSERT Serves 4

Prunes from Agen in France are considered the finest of dried plums but of course you can use any prunes for this dish. California produces some excellent examples.

16 Agen prunes	4 mint sprigs
100 ml armagnac	4 large glasses
400 ml vanilla ice cream	

Stone the prunes, place in a small pan, pour over the armagnac, cover and gently warm through. Leave to cool.

Build up the dessert in the glass in layers — prune, ice cream, prune, ice cream — finishing with prunes on top and garnishing with a sprig of mint.

Serve with biscotti, langues de chat or some shortbread.

Left The entrance
to the Chop House
from the Thames
quayside. On the
right is the kitchen
that prepares gutsy
British bar food:
soups, sausages,
bacon, kidney, and
bubble and squeak.
Opposite page:
Right Plan of the
Chop House; Far
right The great British
classic, sausages
and mash –
superlative British
ingredients beautifully
cooked and served.

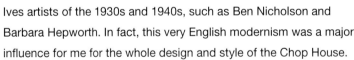

THE BUTLERS WHARF
Chop House

The Butlers Wharf Chop House is exactly the sort of restaurant you'd expect to find in the old Victorian warehouses that line the river by Tower Bridge. First opened in October 1993, it is still the only London restaurant serving traditional British food in modern surroundings.

British food can be, but sadly rarely is, the best in the world. We have cheeses that contend with any made in France and cream of sublime quality and flavour. Our wild game is superlative. Our vegetables and fruit can be tender and delicious (you can't beat English asparagus or apples). From our rivers and coastlines comes an amazing variety of fish and crustacea. Who has ever tasted lobsters, crabs and langoustines better than those from Scotland or Devon? In season our oysters are unbeatable.

It was this huge and undervalued cornucopia that inspired me to demonstrate that British food, sensitively prepared and cooked, really could be delicious. I set about designing a restaurant that would have a thoroughly British feel, somewhere between a cricket pavilion and a boathouse. Like the other restaurants at Butlers Wharf, it was to be on the quayside, right in the shadow of Tower Bridge. We constructed a glass canopy with teapot spouts to drain off the rain, and along the whole length of the restaurant are white painted doors that can be folded back when it is warm and sunny.

Inside, the Chop House is quite woody: there is an oak floor and the banquettes have springy slatted ash backs and ox-blood leather seats. The chairs, with shaped elm seats and ash frames, are inspired by chairmakers, the bodgers of High Wycombe, and the tables are English oak. Close to the entrance to the main restaurant is a vast marble-top table. Today we use it for cutting our excellent bread, but once it was used for pastry-making in the kitchens at Hampton Court. The entrance to the main kitchen has a powerful mural, inspired by the St Ives artists of the 1930s and 1940s, such as Ben Nicholson and Barbara Hepworth. In fact, this very English modernism was a major influence for me for the whole design and style of the Chop House.

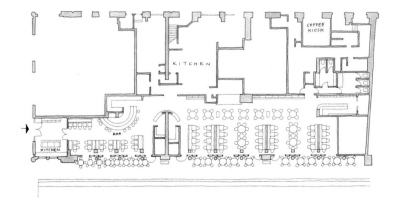

So, what will you eat in the Chop House? It might be classic dishes such as steak and kidney pudding (curiously popular throughout the year), fresh salmon or sea trout, the best English asparagus, sausage and mash, a perfect pork pie, and, of course, really good roast beef, lamb or venison. And don't forget English strawberries with Devonshire cream, Scottish raspberries, or the real delight of a summer pudding or, in winter, spotted dick.

A celebration of traditional British food

Far left, top Simple china, linen, and cutlery – the quintessential Chop House style. **Far left, bottom** The mural at the kitchen entrance, inspired by the St Ives school of British Modernism. **Above** The marble-topped kitchen table from Hampton Court. **Opposite page: Top left** A view across the river to Tower Bridge, with a glass of wine; **Bottom left** A detail of the restaurant interior with fielded oak panels and ash and elm stick-back chairs.; **Top right** The oak bookcase at the back of the restaurant acts as a service station for the waiters as well as a display for British 'below-stairs' china and cooking utensils; **Bottom right** Sitting outside with your feet almost in the river.

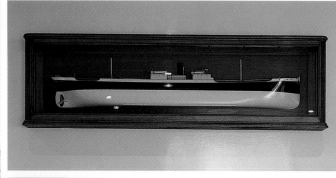

Classic wooden design dominates the Chop House Bar

Above, far left Oak floors and marble-topped tables help create the perfect understated style for a relaxing meal. **Above, top left** Shipyard model of the type of boat that used to be moored alongside the Chop House quay. **Above, bottom left** The simple. brightly lit bar kitchen. **Above, right** The white-painted doors and tongue-and-grooved ceiling are reminiscent of a boathouse or cricket pavilion. **Opposite, main picture** The curved oak TGV front to the zinc-topped bar: the solid oak stools were specially designed for the Chop House.

A destination restaurant for those wanting to experience the best of British food, with a marvellous view of Tower Bridge and the Thames. Here you will find traditional dishes cooked to perfection and the pleasure of fresh seasonal produce.

Recipes from Chop House

CHEF: Andrew Rose   MANAGER: Sean Gavin

Potted Morecambe Bay Shrimps

STARTER Serves 6 generously

500 g poached and peeled brown shrimps	pinch cayenne pepper
180 g butter	pinch sea salt
zest and juice of 1 small lemon	pinch ground black pepper
2 pinches mace	1 tbsp Worcestershire sauce
pinch nutmeg	3 lemons, to serve

Put 50 g of the shrimps with all the other ingredients into a small, heavy-based pan. Over a low heat, gently warm until the butter has melted and started to bubble. Remove from the heat and blitz in a food processor for 30 seconds. Pass through a fine sieve into a bowl, making sure all the butter is pressed through.

Stir in the rest of the shrimps to ensure an even coating, then divide between 6 ramekins. Chill for an hour. Serve straight from the fridge with lots of warm toast and lemon halves.

Steak and Kidney Pudding with Oysters

MAIN Serves 6

500 g plain flour	400 ml Guinness
250 g beef suet	1 bay leaf
2 tsp sea salt	400 ml veal jus (or a
1 tsp baking powder	well-flavoured
filling	chicken stock)
1 kg chuck steak	18 oysters, removed
500 g ox kidney	from their shells
3 tbsp peanut or sunflower oil	(optional)
1 large onion, thinly sliced	

Make the suet crust. Put the flour in a bowl with the suet, baking powder and salt. Stir and work the mixture with a fork, slowly adding just enough water to form a soft dough, but be careful not to overwork it. Cover with cling film and refrigerate whilst making the meat filling.

Cut the beef into 2.5-cm dice. Season and flour the diced steak to coat. Over a medium heat and in a frying pan, brown the meat all over in the oil. Transfer the meat to a saucepan. Fry the sliced onions in the rest of the oil and add them to the meat.

Bring the Guinness to the boil and pour over the meat, adding the bay leaf and veal jus. Simmer gently for 40 minutes until the meat is tender but still firm, as the final steaming process finishes cooking the meat.

Cut the kidney into 2.5-cm dice. Put the kidney dice in a separate pan, cover with cold water and a dash of malt vinegar, bring to the boil and refresh under cold running water. This cleans the kidney and moderates the strong flavour.

Add the kidney to the meat and season with Worcestershire sauce. Leave to cool.

Line 6 x 600-ml pudding basins with cling film. Roll out the suet crust to 4-mm thick, and line the basins with it, reserving enough for the tops. Fill each to the top with the steak and kidney mix, topping up with gravy as required. Dampen the edges of the pastry with a little cold water and cover with the tops, pressing down firmly to seal the edges. Trim off any excess. Cover the puddings with cling film and steam for an hour.

Turn out onto warmed plates, making an incision in the top of each pudding and slipping in 3 oysters. Pour over a little more gravy before serving.

Treacle Pudding and Custard

DESSERT Serves 6

	custard:
30 g butter	
115 g caster sugar	575 ml milk
2 eggs	¼ vanilla pod
170 g flour	7 egg yolks
2 tsp baking powder	30 g caster sugar
1–2 tbsp milk	
55 g golden syrup	

Cream the butter and sugar together, then slowly beat in the egg yolks, one at a time. Sift the flour and baking powder together and fold into the batter, adding milk a tablespoon at a time until you have a dropping consistency.

Butter a 1-kg pudding basin, then pour the syrup into the base. Pour and spoon the mixture to fill the mould three-quarters full. Cover the top with a round of buttered, greaseproof paper, then crimp foil onto cover. Stand in a pan of simmering water, cover with a lid and steam for 1½ hours. Check from time to time, adding boiling water from the kettle as required.

Put on a pan of water to cook the custard over, bringing it to a simmer, that is just below a full boil. In another pan, bring the milk to the boil with the vanilla. Whisk the egg yolks and sugar together in a bowl, then whisk in the hot milk. Put the bowl over the simmering water and stir until you have a coating consistency, that is, when the custard coats the back of a spoon. Pass through a sieve into another bowl, and put this over the hot water to keep warm.

Serve the pudding in slices with the custard poured around.

Above Cantina's simple interior: maplewood table tops, chairs with rush seats, and a wooden model of Tower Bridge resting on a sandbank, all overlooked by an angled mirror. **Opposite page: Right** Plan of Cantina; **Far right** A chef at work in the white-tiled pizza kitchen.

CANTINA
DEL PONTE

A visit to Morocco, a holiday in Provence and memories of the food markets of Venice, plus a re-reading of Elizabeth David's *Mediterranean Food*, all conspired to give me a clear idea of what I wanted to achieve at Cantina, which was to be our third restaurant to benefit from the unique riverfront location by Tower Bridge.

The chefs and kitchens at Cantina produce simple, robust, gutsy food of a kind that you might find in any seaside restaurant or café along the Mediterranean coast. Cantina is a totally unpretentious affair, and very simply designed. On sunny summer days the full-length glazed doors are opened up onto the riverside terrace, which is defined by a border of plane trees growing in bright-yellow tubs. A large turquoise-blue canopy and a terracotta sail protect customers from sudden summer squalls and showers.

The interior of the restaurant is dominated by a magnificent mural painted by Timna Woollard. It's a glorious kaleidoscope of Mediterranean dockside life – the unloading of sailing barges, the vibrant colours of the marketplace, with stalls selling fish, meats, vegetables, cheeses and oils – of the hustle and bustle of kitchens, where steam, flames and smoke rise from pans and stoves and cooks are busy baking breads or making pasta, and finally of the Cantina itself with its huge barrels of wine. If you look at the mural and then close your eyes, it's not hard to imagine that you're on a Venetian canal and not beside the Thames at all! The great thing about the mural is that it gives an accurate description of what you might expect to eat at Cantina. It's a constant inspiration for the chefs – it's their visual cookbook.

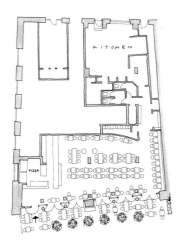

But the first thing you see on entering the restaurant is a cook preparing pizza dough on a white marble table. Nearby are ovens set into the wall and a simple tiled bar with an espresso coffee machine, bottles of good, simple country wine, and generous displays of Mediterranean vegetables – tomatoes, peppers, and courgettes. Wooden-top tables and rush-seated wooden chairs are arranged on the Moroccan terracotta-tiled floor. A simplified wooden model of Tower Bridge lies on a huge sandbank contained by a glass shelf, dominating the end of the restaurant and set above a blue canvas bench seat. The lighting is mainly sited in the ceiling, but six lights like fishing rods illuminate the central aisle.

The china is white, plain and heavy, and the food is exactly what you'd expect having seen the mural – fresh, simple and packed with intense Mediterranean flavours. Think: wonderful pizzas and breads, bottles of robust wine, good espresso coffee and, to wash it all down, a generous grappa.

A taste of the Mediterranean by the Thames

Above, left The small pizza kitchen and its acrobatic chef. **Above, right** Pizzas at Cantina are the real thing: simple, well-baked crusts with gutsy, fresh toppings. **Left** Timna Woollard's beautiful mural of an Italian dockside market runs the full length of the back of the restaurant. **Opposite page: Top left** The mural acts as a spectacular backdrop to the restaurant, helping to create its unique relaxed, informal atmosphere; **Top right** The fully glazed doors open onto a sun-drenched terrace and the glistening river beyond; **Below** A pale-blue canopy and bright-yellow tree tubs help give the impression of blue skies and sunlight even on London's greyest days.

Vibrant detail at the Cantina

Opposite page Teak-top tables team up with
rattan and aluminium outdoor chairs on the
terrace, while a terracotta sail protects
customers from occasional riverside breezes.
Above The service bar in the pizza kitchen is
also used to dispense wine and bread. **Right,
top to bottom:** The eye-catching Cantina
graphics set the right gutsy note; Food is served
on plain white plates that are thick enough to
hold their heat or keep their cool when chilled;
The cheerful take-away menu.

Recipes from Cantina

CHEF: Justin West   MANAGER: Mark Belton

Mozzarella di Bufala with Figs, Mint and Basil

STARTER Serves 4

The fresher your mozzarella, the better. Most mozzarella today is made from cow's milk, though mozzarella made from water-buffalo milk is superior in both taste and texture.

4 balls of buffalo mozzarella	200 g rocket leaves
8 ripe figs	3 tbsp olive oil
1 small bunch basil	juice of half a lemon
1 small bunch mint	salt and pepper

Cut the mozzarella balls and figs into quarters, and combine in a bowl with the basil, mint and rocket leaves. Toss with the olive oil and a squeeze of lemon juice. Arrange on four plates, seasoning with salt and pepper. Serve immediately or the mint and basil will go soggy.

Essentially Italian, Cantina also embraces other Mediterranean influences – all the delicious food of the sun. Situated on Butlers Wharf, the restaurant enjoys a perfect view of the Thames and Tower Bridge.

Scallops with Pancetta, New Potatoes and Broad Beans

MAIN Serves 4

The rich flesh of the scallops is nicely offset by the salty pancetta which also provides the textural contrast in this dish.

1 kg new potatoes peeled and cooked	8 mint leaves
	8 basil leaves
4 spring onions	
50 ml olive oil	1 tbsp olive oil
salt and pepper	12 king scallops
115 g broad beans, shelled and cooked	12 thin slices pancetta (No. 1 cut)

Ask your fishmonger to remove the scallops from the shell.

Make the potato mixture. In a pan over a low-to-medium heat, warm the potatoes with the olive oil. Crush with a fork, before adding the spring onions, broad beans, mint and basil. Season with salt and pepper.

In a frying pan over a medium heat, cook the pancetta on both sides until crisp. Remove and and drain on kitchen paper.

Increase the temperature until the pan is smoking hot, add a little oil and sear the scallops for about 90 seconds each side. The scallops will turn a golden colour.

To serve, spoon the potato mixture into the centre of four warmed plates, arranging the scallops and pancetta around the edge.

Tiramisu

DESSERT Serves 4

An enduring favourite, this must be Italy's best-loved dessert. The quality of the espresso coffee and of the Marsala are what distinguish the best versions.

1 packet Italian sponge fingers	2 eggs
	¼ cup sugar
150 ml espresso or very strong black coffee	1 tbsp hot water
	400 g mascarpone
Marsala	cocoa powder or chocolate, to serve

In a large bowl, place half the sponge fingers and soak them with half the coffee and a good splash of Marsala. The biscuits should retain a 'bite' in the middle.

Separate the egg whites from the yolks. Whip the yolks in a food processor with half the sugar and a tablespoon of hot water. The mixture should treble in volume.

Whip the egg whites in a clean, dry bowl with the remaining sugar, then fold in the egg yolks and mascarpone. Spoon half of this mix onto the soaked biscuits. Place more biscuits on top and soak them with the rest of the coffee and another splash of Marsala. Spoon over the rest of the mixture, smooth over and refrigerate. Before serving, dust the top with good-quality cocoa powder or some grated chocolate.

Above Light and shade: the Coq d'Argent, sited in gardens on top of James Stirling's No.1 Poultry makes brilliant use of the space – no less than five outdoor terraces surround the main restaurant. **Right** Plan of the restaurant and terraces. **Far right** Anthony Caro's cockerel stands guard.

COQ d'ARGENT

No.1 Poultry, bang in the middle of the City of London, is the address of one of the world's quirkiest buildings. Sir James Stirling's last great masterpiece, on the site of a treasure trove of Roman remains and, more recently, of the headquarters of silversmiths Mappin and Webb, lies adjacent to the Bank of England, with commanding views of many other distinguished City institutions.

Peter Palumbo had battled for many years to build on this site, and when he eventually got permission, he offered me this remarkable rooftop garden site as a restaurant. Without hesitation, I agreed. Zoom up to the eighth floor in a space-age lift and you burst out into an astonishingly beautiful garden, designed by Arabella Lennox-Boyd.

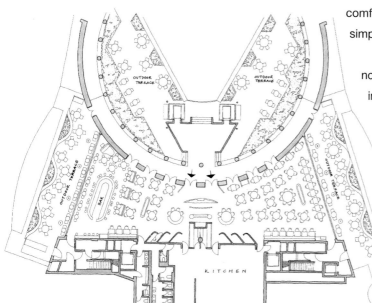

I always feel like Mole greeting the spring in *Wind in the Willows* when I arrive. The garden's two central terraces are surrounded by a huge oak pergola planted with wisteria and vines. Vibrant flowering shrubs such as camellias and buddleia jostle in the borders with scented herbs such as lavender and rosemary. There is even a 90-foot lawn, which in summer becomes the City's picnic ground, littered with blankets and champagne buckets.

The restaurant is divided in two by the central reception desk, on which perches a large, shiny steel cockerel by Anthony Caro. To the right is the bar with its own terrace, which includes an outside grill, while to the left is the more formal restaurant, which also has its outside terrace and a canopy like a spinnaker sail. To this thoroughly modern space, I have tried to give a certain resonance of a gentleman's club. French walnut walls, a floor of Jura limestone and a cigar-brown carpet are joined by comfortable green leather carver chairs, mocha upholstered banquettes and simple square or round tables covered with white linen.

The inspiration for the food and wine comes from Burgundy and northern France. The food is robust and simple and relies on first-rate ingredients. Inevitably, *coq au vin* and roast Bresse chicken are a favourite, along with snails, frogs' legs, the best foie gras with sauterne jelly, and, of course, oysters, lobsters and other crustacea.

On warm summer evenings the Coq, as it is affectionately called, becomes packed with city boys and girls drinking champagne and jugs of Pimm's. Nevertheless, in this brilliantly organized space, it is still possible to have a quiet, romantic dinner for two.

Rooftop dining at the heart of the City

Above, left A spinnaker-like canopy and outdoor heaters protect diners even on somewhat chilly days and nights. **Above, right** A crustacea counter decorated with a mosaic of waves and shells dispenses seafood. **Below, left** Vines add a touch of bacchanalian lushness to the terraces. **Opposite page: Top left** Dining alfresco seems to be something of a passion for people usually ensconced in air-conditioned offices; **Bottom left** Curved walnut walls and leather carver chairs give the Coq a rather clubby feel; **Top right** The Apex Terrace has become the City's favourite picnic spot; **Bottom right** A large oval bar adjacent to one of the terraces with its own outdoor grill is a major attraction.

Sterling luxury

Above The Coq's graphics are inspired by a silver hallmark. **Right** Walnut screens with integral lighting divide the bar from the restaurant. **Top, right** China, glass, cutlery and even the salt and pepper grinders were specially designed. **Opposite page: Top, left** A dish of lobster served on crushed ice sums up the combination of simplicity and luxury that is typical of the Coq's food; **Top, right** Caro's steel cockerel; **Below, left** One of the outside terraces, with walls of Helidon sandstone and Cornish red sandstone; **Far right** The Coq's special hallmarked ashtrays are designed with cigar smokers in mind.

Recipes from Coq d'Argent

CHEF: Mickael Weiss MANAGER: Antoine Melon

King Scallop Gratin

STARTER Serves 4

4 extra-large (king)
    scallops, cleaned
    and on the half
    shell
1 shallot, thinly sliced
100 g button
    mushrooms
20 g butter
20 ml dry white wine
juice of half a lemon
100 g mussels,
    cooked and
    shelled

100 g prawns,
    cooked and
    shelled
1 tbsp parsley, finely
    chopped
1 tbsp chives, thinly
    cut
white sauce:
30 g butter
30 g flour
450 ml milk
2 egg yolks
salt and pepper

Ask your fishmonger to prepare the scallops for you, keeping the coral intact. Reserve the scallops, and boil the shells for 5 minutes to clean them.

Sweat the shallots and mushrooms in the butter until soft. Add the white wine and lemon juice, and bring to the boil. Remove from the heat and stir in the mussels, prawns and herbs.

In a pan, melt the butter, add the flour and cook for 2 minutes over a low heat, stirring with a wooden spoon. Add the milk and season with salt and pepper. Bring to the boil, then simmer for 4 minutes. Add the egg yolks and mushrooms. Cook, stirring, until it thickens and remove from the heat.

Preheat an overhead grill to very hot.

Over a medium-to-high heat, heat a heavy-based frying pan to smoking hot. Brush the scallops with a little oil and sear them briefly on both sides before returning them to the cleaned shells. Pour the sauce mixture over the top, then place under the grill for 5 minutes or until bubbling hot and golden. Serve immediately on warmed plates.

Coq au Vin

MAIN Serves 4

8 corn-fed chicken
    legs
1 litre red wine
1 carrot, peeled and
    diced
1 onion, peeled and
    diced
1 stick of celery,
    diced
1 spring of thyme
1 garlic clove
1 bay leaf
500 ml chicken stock
flour
salt and pepper

100 g unsmoked
    streaky bacon, cut
    in lardons
200 g button
    mushrooms
12 baby onions,
    peeled
2 slices white bread,
    crusts removed
    and cut in 1-cm
    dice
2–3 tbsp olive oil
1 garlic clove, peeled
    and chopped
handful flat-leaf
    parsley, chopped

Cut the chicken legs into two through the joint, separating the drumsticks from the thighs. Marinate the chicken with the diced vegetables, herbs and wine in the refrigerator overnight or for 6 hours at room temperature.

Preheat the oven to 170 °C.

Dry the chicken legs on a kitchen towel. Flour lightly and brown them in a casserole dish. Pour the marinade with its vegetables over the chicken, bring to the boil and add the stock. Bake in the oven uncovered for 50–60 minutes.

Fry the lardons until they colour and release fat. Add the mushrooms and onions, stirring to coat and cooking to take colour. Add to the casserole 10 minutes before serving.

Put the olive oil and garlic in a bowl. Turn the bread to coat, then fry in an unoiled pan over a low temperature, turning frequently until crisp and brown.

To serve, sprinkle the top with the croutons and garnish with chopped parsley.

Tarte Tatin

DESSERT Serves 4

1.35 kg Golden
    Delicious apples
85 g caster sugar

60 g unsalted butter
500 g frozen
    butter puff pastry

Peel and core the apples and cut in quarters.

Put the sugar into a shallow pan or heavy frying pan with an oven-proof handle and put over a low heat to caramelize. To prevent burning, turn the pan from time to time to distribute the heat evenly. Take the sugar to a dark caramel, but be careful not to take it too far. If it burns then you must throw it away and start again or it will be bitter. When you judge the caramel is ready, remove the pan from the heat.

Dot the surface of the caramel with small pieces of butter and pack the quartered apples tightly on top, filling any gaps with wedges of apple. They shrink during cooking, so the tighter you pack them, the better.

Preheat the oven to 190 °C.

Dot the top of the apples with butter and put the pan back on a low heat for 3–5 minutes to melt the caramel and start the apples cooking.

Roll out the pastry to a thickness of about 1 cm, and using a plate with the same circumference as the pan as a template, cut in a circle. Fold in half and lay on top of the apples and unfold to cover, tucking the edges of the pastry inside the pan.

Bake for 30–35 minutes when the apples will be cooked and the pastry puffed and golden. Leave to cool for 10 minutes. Cover the top of the pan with an upside-down serving plate and invert. Sit the plate on a flat surface, rap the bottom of the pan and remove.

Serve while still warm, with crème fraîche or with vanilla ice cream.

Real French food in the heart of the City, the Coq has a roof terrace as well as an elegant dining room overlooking the financial district. Foie gras, snails, delicate fish dishes and robust regional meat classics – all are cooked authentically here.

Left The stained-glass dome of the Aurora restaurant is the most outstanding of the grand Victorian details we discovered in the abused and neglected fabric of the Great Eastern, and which now contribute to the elegant atmosphere of this thoroughly contemporary hotel. **Opposite page** The handsome stairwell to the GE club descends to the entrance of the Terminus bar.

When I first saw the Great Eastern some five years ago, I thought it was one of the most depressing and derelict places that I had ever come across. The building seemed symbolic of everything that had been wrong with England in the post-war years. Its only real claim to fame was that you could rent rooms by the hour, and everything else about the place seemed to reflect this seediness. It had been built in the 1880s as a grand hotel attached to Liverpool Street Railway Station. The architecture was High Victorian, its imposing grandeur reflecting the glamour of travel and the boundless confidence felt by the British of that time about their position in the world.

When we and our partners first faced the daunting challenge of how to bring this defunct anachronism into the twenty-first century, we immediately decided that some major reorientation and reconstruction would be needed. We realized, too, that this would be to some extent hampered by the listed nature of some of the hotel's fairly second-rate Victorian architecture and interior details. How, then, could we make the new Great Eastern into a thoroughly contemporary hotel – in fact, the only hotel in the City of London – one that would bridge the City world of high finance with the blossoming creative areas of Shoreditch, Clerkenwell and Hoxton?

To achieve this, we undertook a fairly radical replanning of the space, creating a vast atrium in the centre pierced by our mini-Guggenheim that connects the six floors of the hotel. We also added a further two floors under a new mansard roof. All 267 bedrooms are different: some in the roof space are modern and have charming round windows; others, on the lower floors, combine Victorian grandeur and spaciousness with modern furnishings. All the rooms are very comfortable and equipped with everything the modern traveller could need.

Perhaps the most notable thing about the new Great Eastern, however, is the restaurants, bars, and cafés grouped around the ground floor, each of them open to the street frontage. Each in its own way is very different to the typical hotel dining room, and all are open to the general public as well as to guests. They are all freestanding entities in their own right and very different to each other in price and in what they offer.

Of the restaurants, the Aurora is the grandest and most classic, with a heavily listed Victorian interior and a huge, magnificent stained-glass dome which we have lit from outside so it glows at night. This quite formal restaurant is designed for business lunches and dinners and is aimed at city executives who want the classic cuisine and service of a grand West End restaurant. It's also a place for parties and celebrations. The food is elegantly

Above, top to bottom Logos for the Aurora and Fishmarket restaurants and the GE Club. We always try to instil in the logo something of the character of the restaurant or bar. **Opposite page, top to bottom** Logos for the George 'pub', Miyabi, and Terminus.

delicious, with an outstanding cheese trolley, a remarkable wine list, and very proper service. Aurora was hailed as the most popular rendezvous in the City when it first opened in 1884, and we hope we will make it that again.

Fish and crustacea have long been a favourite fare of the City, and Fishmarket, with its excellent restaurant and champagne and oyster bar, satisfies this appetite admirably. Our fish is cooked very simply and serves as a reminder that Britain's shores and rivers provide us with an abundance of delicious produce that can almost jump onto our plates without too much help from the kitchen. There are plates of grilled turbot and halibut, huge platters of Dover sole, pints of prawns, mounds of oysters, piles of langoustines, lobsters hot with butter or cold with mayonnaise, and glistening towers of all kinds of *fruits de mer*.

The main restaurant at Fishmarket is a listed room, featuring stained glass, creamy marble and original chandeliers as the outstanding grace notes. The new crustacea altar with its mosaic front provides a focal point for the preparation of the truly superlative *plateau de fruits de mer*. The furnishings are simple, with curved screens and banquettes defining the space.

The huge, oval champagne and oyster bar sits in the middle of a grand room encrusted with dark plaster mouldings. Here, 25 different champagnes and vintages, in quantities ranging from half-bottles to magnums, and even jeroboams and methuselahs, are consumed, together with vast platters of oysters – quite often to celebrate deals but sometimes just to speed the journey home. A pint of Guinness with a simple plate of oysters is a very palatable alternative, especially if there is nothing particular to celebrate.

The GE Club is the members-only private space at the Great Eastern. It's a long thin room, with a huge cigar humidor close to the entrance and a padded red-leather bar at one end. The central corridor has a wide walnut floor, which at night, when the music is at full blast, can be filled with jiggling couples. Normally, though, this is a calm and comfortable room. There are large modern chairs and banquettes, flattering lighting and a changing exhibition of pictures, reflecting the work of local artists or photographers. Try to get a member of the club to invite you up for a drink and to smoke a Havana!

George is really our railway pub, and here, as you would expect, pints of beer and stout are the usual tipple. Food is of the traditional comfort kind combined with a modern twist and includes pies, English sausages, roast-beef or ham sandwiches, ploughman's platters of cheddar cheese and pickles, and, to finish, treacle and summer puddings – all good, hearty stuff.

The interior of George is extraordinary, epitomizing the late-Victorian predilection for historical pastiche. Its oak-panelled walls and decorative plaster ceiling make it one of the finest 'Tudorbethan' interiors in London. To this we have added a large simple bar, solid-oak tables and stools that, while modern, seem to work well in this rather florid setting.

Miyabi is a tiny 28-seat restaurant serving really excellent sushi, sashimi and tempura. Most of the cooking is done at the counter in front of the customers. The restaurant also provides a bento-box service, used not only by the many Japanese employees who now work in the City but also by the Europeans, who over the last few years have developed a taste for the elegant freshness and healthiness of Japanese food – I certainly have!

The interior looks very Japanese and, at the same time, very modern. The traditional architecture of Japan has been very influential on many Modernist and Post-modern architects and designers, from Frank Lloyd Wright to David Chipperfield. There was a lot of competition in our design office for the job of working on this serenely simple space. Personally I very much enjoyed designing the restaurant's tables and chairs.

And there is Terminus, the bustling bar and brasserie that should be a part of every thriving railway terminal, but which has become the decaying station buffet you experience in most British stations. While remaining entirely British, Terminus aims to recapture something of the glamour and charm of the Gare du Nord or the Gare de Lyon in Paris. Its huge well-stocked bar, cast-iron columns and bentwood chairs and tables are just right for a place that serves breakfast, lunch and supper and doesn't close until the last train leaves the station.

The simple menu is spot-on, too: at lunch and suppertime there are grills and our own special beefburgers, risottos, pastas and club sandwiches, with, perhaps, a green Thai curry as a spicy surprise; there are croissants and Danish in the morning, and pastries in the afternoon. There's plenty of beer, a well-chosen but simple wine list, and plenty of champagne and cocktails for the City boys and girls who make this such a busy, lively and rather noisy place at times.

AUROPA

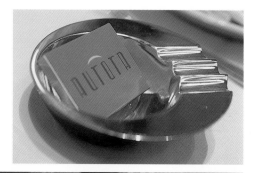

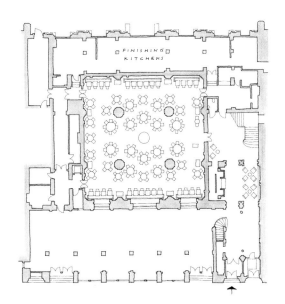

Above Plan of Aurora, one of London's grandest restaurants **Above, right** The Aurora ashtray, with its echo of the restaurant's crescent symbol. **Right** The restaurant's specially designed dining chairs and wine bucket and stand. **Opposite page: Main picture** The central waiters' station and flower display acts as a spectacular focal point; **Far right, top to bottom** The street entrance; An illuminated menu box; A special chocolate treat.

Victorian pomp and circumstance clothed in modern style

Above, left Waiters carry out much of the service from *guéridon* tables. **Above, right** The embroidered antimacassars on the backs of the dining chairs refer to the hotel's railway heritage. **Opposite page** The listed Victorian columns, mouldings and stained-glass dome combine with the simple furniture, marble and mosaic floor, and the translucent porcelain chandeliers to create a grand yet modern restaurant.

The high-ceilinged dining-room with dramatic glass cupola provides a distinguished backdrop for Aurora's sophisticated and elegant cooking.

Recipes from Aurora

CHEF: Robert Stirrup MANAGER Simon Newson

Raviolis of Langoustine with Tomato and Courgettes

STARTER Serves 4

200 g spinach leaves	1 tbsp olive oil
8 langoustines	½ garlic clove, peeled
50 g shallots, finely	and finely chopped
chopped	4 coriander leaves,
2 tbsp olive oil	finely chopped
50 g courgettes,	2 basil leaves, finely
diced	chopped
2 small tomatoes,	½ tsp caster sugar
blanched, peeled	**garnish:**
and diced	100 g tomatoes,
2 basil leaves, finely	peeled, de-seeded
chopped	and diced
200 g fresh pasta	1 tbsp olive oil
herb vinaigrette:	salt and pepper
heads and shells	
from langoustines	

Bring a large pan of salted water to a fast boil. Blanch the spinach leaves in the water for 10 seconds, removing immediately to iced water to stop further cooking. Drain.

Blanch the langoustines in the same boiling water for 1–2 minutes then transfer to iced water. Remove, drain and remove the tails. Peel off the shells, and cut the flesh into dice. Reserve with the claws.

In a heavy-based frying pan, sweat the shallots in olive oil for 1 minute. Add the courgettes and cook, stirring, for another minute. Add the langoustines and stir-fry briefly, then add the tomatoes, basil and coriander. Season, remove from the heat and leave to cool.

Fry the langoustine shells in the olive oil for 10 seconds. Add the garlic, the sugar and a little salt and pepper. Add 75 ml water, bring to the boil and remove immediately from the heat. Leave to infuse for 15 minutes. Pass through a fine sieve. Add the basil and coriander.

Mix the spinach with the langoustine mixture and divide into 20 spoonfuls.

Using a 10-cm pastry cutter, cut out 20 rounds of pasta and brush the edges with cold water. Spoon the filling onto the bottom half of the rounds. Fold and press the edges together to make a tight seal. Bring the ends back together.

Put the raviolis in boiling salted water for a minute, then simmer for 4 minutes. Drain.

Warm the garnish in olive oil. Place the tomatoes in the centre of each plate, circle with the raviolis and spoon the vinaigrette around.

Veal Sweetbreads with Watercress

MAIN Serves 4

4 x 200-g veal	1 egg yolk
sweetbreads,	40 g cold unsalted
soaked under	butter, diced
running water for	**garnish:**
2 hours	1 carrot, diced
30 g unsalted butter	1 courgette, diced
sauce:	1 small celery stalk,
3 shallots, chopped	diced
10ml dry sherry	1 large white
100g watercress	mushroom cap,
leaves	diced
10ml chicken stock	20 g unsalted butter
1tbsp cream	salt and pepper

Preheat the oven to 220 °C.

Bring a pan of water to the boil and blanch the sweetbreads for 30 seconds. Remove to iced water for 30 seconds and then dry. Melt the butter. Add the sweetbreads and brown for about 2 minutes. Put them on a tray and brush with melted butter. Season with salt and pepper and roast for 15 minutes. Remove and leave to rest for 10 minutes, loosely covered with foil.

Put a tablespoon of water in a small pan, bring to the boil with a teaspoon of butter.

Season, add the diced carrots, cook for a minute, add the courgettes, celery and mushrooms, cook for a further minute. Reserve.

Sweat the chopped shallots until soft and transparent. Turn up the heat, deglaze with the sherry and reduce by half. Add the chicken stock, bring to the boil and sieve into a pan.

Bring to the boil, then add the watercress. Whisk together the cream and egg yolk and stir into the chicken and watercress liquid, whisking until it thickens. Finally, whisk in the diced cold butter, until incorporated. Do not allow it to boil or the sauce will split. Add the vegetables and the cooking juices released by the sweetbreads.

Warm the sweetbreads in the oven for a few minutes, then arrange them in the centre of large warmed plates and pour the sauce around.

Chocolate and Caramel Tart

DESSERT Makes a 25-cm tart

225 g caster sugar	**chocolate filling:**
100 ml spring water	170 g bittersweet
150 ml single cream	chocolate,
115 g unsalted	chopped
butter, cut into dice	30 g unsalted butter
25-cm pastry tart	
case, baked blind	

Make the caramel. Put the sugar and water in a heavy-based saucepan and bring to the boil. Lower the heat and slowly take it to 180 °C on a sugar thermometer. Remove from the heat and add the cream, a spoonful at a time. When all the cream has been incorporated, gradually stir in the butter to give a smooth sauce. Pour into the tart case and leave to set.

Melt the chocolate in a bowl set over water. Remove from the heat and beat in the butter. Spread over the set caramel with a plastic spatula. Leave to cool before serving.

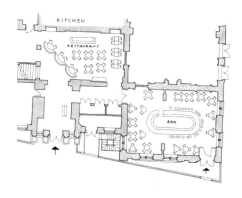

Top, left Plan of the restaurant and bar
Top, right The street entrance to Fishmarket
Bottom, left The leaping fish symbol on a
coffee cup. **Bottom, right** An exquisite flower
arrangement on the bar. **Opposite page** The
restaurant's beautiful listed interior is graced by
elegant marble walls and columns and fine
stained glass. Dark oak screens-cum-banquettes
define the space.

Champagne and crustacea for aficionados

Top, left The back-lit original stained-glass windows provide a stunning backdrop for the elegant towers of crustacea. **Above** The oyster and champagne bar is dominated by its huge central counter; the oyster end of the bar is covered in mosaic that has been designed to look like bubbling water. **Bottom, left** Champagne cools on the bar. **Opposite page: Left** The reception desk with the leaping-fish symbol on the floor; **Right** The serious champagne-drinkers end of the bar.

At the sign of the leaping fish

Opposite page Bold, eye-catching menu graphics: a uniform graphic style and subtle use of a logo help create an overall feel of well-tended luxury. **Above, left** The Fishmarket graphic in mosaic set in the stone floor. **Above, right** More leaping fish! **Left** The dark-brown background created by the Victorian mouldings contrasts with the simple modern furniture. **Right** Sugar for coffee – tiny details matter.

As the name suggests, the emphasis at
Fishmarket is on the freshest fish, cooked
simply and sensitively. The wine list reflects this
and also includes many fine champagnes.

Recipes from Fishmarket

CHEF: Stuart Lyall MANAGER: Stephan Baron

Potato Pancakes with Smoked Eel

STARTER Serves 4

500 g potatoes, peeled weight	¼ nutmeg, grated
60 g flour	1 tbsp sunflower oil
125 ml milk	300 g smoked eel fillets, skin removed
2 eggs	
3 egg whites	1 leafy lemon

Boil and mash the potatoes. Return to the hot pan and shake until dry before beating in the flour. Whisk the milk with 2 eggs and 3 egg whites and beat into the potato to form a thick, smooth batter. Season with salt, pepper and a grating of nutmeg. Stand for 10 minutes.

Heat a crêpe pan to smoking-hot then film the base with sunflower oil, wiping out any excess with a paper towel. Pour in a quarter of the batter and turn down the heat slightly. Cook for about 3 minutes, before turning. Transfer to a warmed plate in a low oven while you cook the rest, wiping the pan with oiled paper for each.

To serve, divide the smoked eel between four plates, putting a pancake beside each portion. Cut the lemon in quarters lengthways, putting a quarter on each plate. Serve while the pancakes are still warm.

Pan-fried Sea Bream with Squid and Provençale Vegetables

MAIN Serves 4

4 ripe plum tomatoes	about 20 threads of saffron
½ tsp thyme	
75 ml olive oil	½ bay leaf
4 x 120-g fillets grey sea bream, pin-boned and skin on	2 cloves garlic, peeled and sliced paper thin

2 tbsp olive oil	2 tsp dried orange zest
cayenne pepper	
150 g squid tubes, cut in thin slices	1 star anise
	100 g sea salt
2 tbsp olive oil	20 g black peppercorns
½ garlic clove, sliced paper thin	
	garnish:
5 marinated baby artichokes	1 tbsp coriander leaves, chopped
1 red onion, cut into 1-cm dice	1 tbsp flat-leaf parsley, chopped
1 tsp dried thyme	1 tbsp lemon juice
seasoning:	½ garlic clove
2 tsp dried thyme	2 slices white bread, crusts removed and cut in 1-cm dice.
2 tsp dried lemon zest, chopped finely	

Grind all the seasoning ingredients together, and keep in a sealed jar.

Preheat the oven to 100 °C.

Brush a tray or roasting tin with olive oil. Cut the tomatoes in half lengthways and place them on the tray, cut surface upwards. Drizzle olive oil over and season with salt, pepper and thyme. Dry in the oven for 4 hours. Reserve.

Make the rouille. Put the saffron to soak in a tablespoon of hot water for 10 minutes. Whisk the garlic and egg yolks. Gradually add the olive oil, whisking. As it thickens, add the saffron and its soaking water. Whisk in the lemon juice and add salt and cayenne pepper to taste.

Sweat the onion with 2 tablespoons of olive oil until soft. Remove and reserve.

Put 2 more tablespoons of olive oil in the pan, and, over a low heat, fry the bread cubes until crisp and golden brown. Drain on kitchen paper.

Heat a heavy-based frying pan until smoking hot. Brush the fillets with olive oil and season. Sear in the pan for 1 minute on each side. Season with salt and a pinch of the seasoning mixture and reserve, skin side up.

Add another tablespoon of olive oil to the pan and stir-fry the squid for 10 seconds. Add the red onion, the quartered artichokes, the parsley, coriander and garlic. Fry for 1 minute, stirring, then add the lemon juice.

To serve, divide the vegetable mixture between four warmed plates, sitting the sea-bream fillets, skin side up, on top. Arrange the roast tomatoes around the fish and scatter the croutons over. Spoon rouille around and serve.

Sherry Trifle

DESSERT Serves 8

1 x 23-cm Victoria sponge	100 g caster sugar
	600 ml full-fat milk
115 g raspberry jam	3 drops of vanilla essence
115 g apricot jam	
100 ml brandy	600 ml whipping cream
100 ml sweet sherry	
custard:	2 tbsp flaked almonds
5 egg yolks	

Split the sponge in half, spreading one half with raspberry jam and the other with apricot jam. Cut each into 4 and put into a dish, alternating raspberry with apricot. Pour over the brandy and the sweet sherry and leave for 2 hours.

Make a custard. Bring a pan of water to the boil. Lower the heat to simmer. In a bowl that will sit on top of the pan over the water, whisk the egg yolks and sugar with an electric whisk until pale and creamy. Bring the milk to the boil in a pan and pour it slowly into the egg and sugar cream, whisking continuously. Put the bowl over the simmering water and whisk until thick. Stir in 3 drops of vanilla essence and pour over the sponge. Refrigerate overnight.

Whip the cream and spoon over the top, scattering over some flaked almonds to finish.

Left The sexy red-leather bar at the GE Club, with specially designed bar stools.
Opposite page Much of the warmth and intimacy of the club derives from its rich walnut floor, which has a curvy stainless-steel inset line running the length of the room. Comfortable chairs and banquette seats are grouped down the sides.

Members only: cocktails and cigars in an intimate setting

Above, left The entrance to this private club is dominated by a huge and handsome humidor filled with the finest Havana cigars. **Above** The atmosphere in the club is very convivial, with excellent night-time music. On the walls is a changing display of art, connecting to the adjacent creative quarters of Hoxton, Spitalfields and Shoreditch in London. **Opposite page: Main picture** The GE Club graphics displayed on an ashtray and bar list; **Bottom, left and right** Cocktails are a speciality.

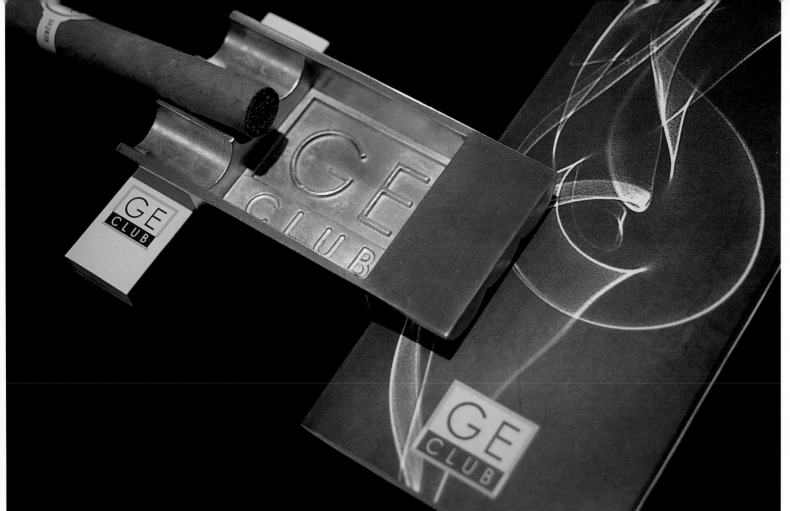

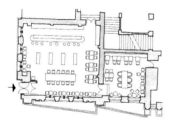

Above Plan of the George. **Top** We nickname this simple annex to the George, reminiscent of a railway waiting room, 'Mildred' in honour of the 1970s sitcom *George and Mildred*. **Bottom, left** Pewter beer mugs and a jar of pickles. **Bottom, right** The Saint George's shield – symbol of the best English beer drinker. **Opposite page** The listed Victorian interior contrasts with the simple oak furniture to make an amusing and popular interior. The food and beer are good, too!

George celebrates great British classic food, all delivered to the most exacting standards – a constant reminder that when done well, this is very good food indeed.

Recipes from George

CHEF: Stuart Lyall MANAGER: James Thompson

Split Pea and Ham Soup

STARTER Serves 6

225 g green split peas	1 onion, peeled
1 small smoked ham shank	3 tbsp chopped flat-leaf parsley
60 g unsalted butter	salt and pepper
4 sticks celery with leaves	12 chives, to garnish

Put the split peas and the ham shank in a pan with 2 litres of water and bring to the boil. Skim, lower the heat to a simmer and cook gently for 30 minutes, stirring occasionally.

Dice the onion and celery and sweat over a low heat with the butter until soft, taking care not to allow it to colour. Chop the parsley and celery leaves then stir into the soup with the onion and celery. Season with plenty of pepper and continue to simmer, stirring at regular intervals and adding more water if it gets too thick or shows signs of sticking. After 30–40 minutes the split peas will have broken down to form a thick purée. Take out the ham shank and set aside to cool.

Pull the ham off the bone and shred. Stir the ham back into the soup.

Ladle into large warmed bowls, scattering some thinly cut chives on top. Serve with crusty bread and butter.

Braised Oxtail with Cauliflower Purée

MAIN Serves 6

2 kg oxtails	2 carrots, peeled
85 g streaky bacon, cut in lardons	3 sticks celery
about 60 g flour	2 garlic cloves, peeled
2 large onions	4 tbsp sunflower or other neutral oil

300 ml red wine	2 tbsp Worcestershire sauce
bouquet garni:	
2 bay leaves, a handful of parsley stalks and a sprig of thyme	500 g chopped tinned tomatoes
	flat-leaf parsley
	salt and pepper

Soak the jointed pieces in iced water for 4 hours to extract blood and impurities then trim off fat.

In a heavy-based frying pan, sweat the bacon in a little oil until it starts to brown and give off its fat. Remove to a large casserole.

Dry the oxtail pieces then dredge in seasoned flour. Add some oil to the bacon fat and brown the oxtail over a medium heat, before adding to the casserole. Pack them in, standing upright in a single layer. Scatter over 30 g more flour.

Chop the onion, carrots, celery and garlic into small dice, add a little more oil to the frying pan and brown them, stirring constantly. Transfer to the casserole. Deglaze the frying pan over a high heat with the wine, incorporating all the burnt bits and pour over the oxtail and vegetables.

Push the bouquet garni down into the centre. Add the Worcestershire sauce and chopped tomatoes, pouring over enough water to cover. Season with salt and pepper. Bring to the boil, skim, then turn down to a bare simmer and cook for 2 hours. Check to see whether the meat is cooked: it's done when it pulls easily off the bone. At this point remove the meat and bacon with a slotted spoon to a plate and reserve, refrigerating when cool. Strain the braising liquid through a sieve into a bowl or plastic container and discard the bouquet garni.

When cool, refrigerate the liquid also. The next day the fat will have set on the surface and can be easily lifted off and discarded. Return the liquid to the hob and cook down to a rich, glossy sauce. Transfer to a food processor and liquidize. Put the oxtail pieces into a pan and

pour the sauce over and round them through a sieve, pressing to extract all the liquid with a wooden spoon. Reheat gently and keep warm.

Serve on large soup plates scattered with lots of chopped parsley and with mashed potatoes or a cauliflower purée.

Sticky Toffee Pudding

DESSERT Serves 4

60 g caster sugar	115 g muscovado sugar
75 ml double cream	
115 g unsalted butter plus a little for the moulds	4 eggs
	140 g plain flour
	1½ tsp baking powder

Preheat the oven to 180 °C.

Butter 4 x 300-ml dariole moulds.

In a pan melt the caster sugar with 2 tbsp of water over a low heat. Warm the cream in another pan. When liquid, turn up the heat under the sugar to medium and boil until golden brown. Remove from the heat and add the hot cream, stirring constantly. Pour equally into the 4 moulds to line the bases.

With an electric whisk, cream the butter and muscovado sugar until off-white and then whisk in 4 egg yolks. In a metal or glass bowl whisk 4 egg whites to a soft peak and reserve.

Sift the flour and baking powder and whisk into the butter cream then fold in the egg whites. Spoon into the moulds and cover the tops with buttered rounds of greaseproof paper then pleated foil to allow for expansion.

Put into a roasting tin and pour hot water from the kettle to come halfway up the moulds and bake for 40–50 minutes, when a skewer pushed into the middle should come out warm and clean.

Serve with warm crème anglaise (*see* p. 137).

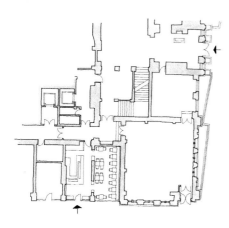

Above Plan of the restaurant **Right** Miyabi graphics make a striking addition to the china, menus, mats and chopstick sleeves. **Opposite page** The cool simplicity of the tiny, neat interior transports you to Japan. The square 'windows' are covered with a metal gauze and are lit from behind. Indirect light floods the wood panelling, giving a mellow glow to the restaurant at night.

Japan in the heart of the City of London

Above, left and right The sushi preparation counter offers a mouth-watering array of beautifully prepared dishes. **Below, left** Sushi depends on the freshest products combined to colourful, striking effect. **Below, right** Many Japanese companies now have offices in the City, and Miyabi has become one of their favourite eating places. **Opposite page: Main picture** The very minimal interior with its mellow light is very atmospheric both at lunch and in the evening; **Bottom** The sushi counter is the hub of the restaurant, where chefs and assistants work hard at preparing and dispensing food and drink. The take-away bento boxes are also sold from here.

Pure food, pure design

Opposite page: Left The 'Mocha' chair and
table, which I designed especially for Miyabi;
Top right The simple, monochrome dishes of the
Conran Collection are ideal for the presentation
of Japanese food; **Bottom right** Even the flowers
are especially chosen to suit the Miyabi style.
This page: Above The mural at Miyabi recalls
Tokyo's extraordinary night-time cityscape;
Below The menu cover comes with an uplifting
message extolling the virtues of Japanese food.

miyabi
'grace and refinement':
of spirit and mind,
taste and texture,
body and soul;
fresh, healthy food;
simplicity and confidence;
now and always

Recipes from Miyabi

CHEF: Naomi Yuzawa MANAGER: Roger Gibbons

Asparagus Ohitashi with Bacon

STARTER Serves 4

In this one dish we find three of the key flavours of Japanese cooking: Kikkoman soy, distinguished by its inclusion of fermented wheat; mirin, a sweet rice wine; and dried bonito flakes.

50 ml Kikkoman soy sauce	500 g asparagus
150 ml fish stock	100 g pancetta or streaky bacon
1 tsp mirin	
3 g dried bonito flakes	

Bring the soy sauce, fish stock, mirin and bonito to the boil. Pour into a container and cool.

Unless they are the first of the season, peel the ends of the asparagus. Bring a pan of salted water to the boil and cook the asparagus for 3–4 minutes or until just done, transferring immediately to a bowl of iced water to stop further cooking.

Dice the bacon, put in a frying pan over a low heat and cook slowly until brown and crispy.

To serve, place the asparagus on a plate, pour over the sauce and sprinkle with the bacon.

Chicken Teriyaki

MAIN Serves 4

Because of the sugar, sake and mirin – respectively, dry and sweet rice wines – it contains, teriyaki sauce is sticky and so can burn easily. Teriyaki is usually grilled, but in this Miyabi version it is cooked in a pan.

400 g chicken legs or thighs, boned	**teriyaki sauce:**
	180 ml soy sauce
2–3 tbsp vegetable oil	50 g sugar
	20 ml sake
	20 ml mirin

Cut the boned chicken into neat pieces.

Heat the oil in a frying pan over a medium heat and brown the chicken on both sides. Lower the heat and cook until just done – about 3 minutes each side. Remove the chicken and reserve in a warm place.

Add the teriyaki ingredients to the pan and cook down for 2–3 minutes. Return the chicken to the pan, coat with the sauce until the chicken is glazed.

To serve, place the chicken on a plate and garnish with shredded fresh vegetables.

Ginger Nama Choco

DESSERT Serves 4–6

150 g stem ginger in syrup	300 g whipping cream
200 g dark chocolate	cocoa powder, for dusting
20 g butter	
20 g glucose	

Put 100 g of the stem ginger in a food processor with 50 ml of the syrup and purée. Reserve.

In a bowl set over a pan of simmering water, melt the chocolate and butter, then stir in the glucose, stirring well. Stir into the chocolate mixture 1 tbsp of the whipping cream to lighten it slightly, then stir in the remaining cream. Add the blended ginger, then pour into a square frame or mould.

When set, cut into squares and serve dusted with cocoa powder and garnished with pieces of stem ginger.

Traditional and modern Japanese dishes,
with a Western slant in the ingredients.

TERMINUS

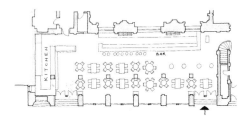

Top left Plan of Terminus **Above** Terminus graphics on the ashtray link it to the railway terminal. **Right, top and bottom** Everything is designed to be easy and informal, including simple bentwood chairs and laminate-topped café tables. **Opposite page** The huge bar is busy from breakfast until the last train leaves Liverpool Street Station. The open kitchen is at the far end.

Terminus is one of the City's busiest restaurants with a long bar that is packed at lunch and dinner. The food here is eclectic, popular with its hundreds of customers and always deliciously simple.

Recipes from Terminus

CHEF: Sydney Aldridge MANAGER: Paula Dupuy

Spiced Parsnip Soup with Coriander Bread

STARTER Serves 4

large bunch fresh coriander	1 tbsp mild curry powder
100 ml olive oil	1 tbsp ground coriander
salt and pepper	1 tbsp ground cumin
1 kg parsnips, peeled	1 litre vegetable stock
1 leek, cleaned and sliced	potato and rosemary bread, or sourdough
1 onion, sliced	
1 stick celery, sliced	
100 g butter	

First make the coriander oil. Blanch the coriander in boiling water for 30 seconds, refresh in cold water and then put in a food processor. Blitz, pouring the olive oil through the feeder tube until you have a smooth purée. Season to taste with salt and pepper.

Roughly dice the parsnips. In a large saucepan, sweat the parsnips, leek, onion and celery in the butter over a medium heat. Add the curry powder, the coriander and cumin, together with some salt and pepper. Cook, stirring with a wooden spoon, for 2–3 minutes, adding a little water if it starts to stick on the bottom of the pan.

Add the vegetable stock, bring to the boil, then bring down the heat and simmer for 20–30 minutes.

Blend and pass through a conical strainer. If it is too thick, thin with a little water. Taste and adjust the seasoning.

Brush the coriander oil onto slices of potato and rosemary bread or sourdough.

Ladle the soup into large warmed bowls and serve with warm coriander bread on the side.

Skate Wing, Baby Gem, Caper and Parsley Butter

MAIN Serves 4

90 g unsalted butter	50 g flat-leaf parsley, retain stalks
8 heads baby gem	100 ml clarified butter
50 g shallots, peeled and sliced	4 x 450-g skate wing
100 ml fish stock	25 ml single cream
250 ml white chicken stock	120 g capers
50 ml white wine	juice of 1 lemon
50 ml white-wine vinegar	

Preheat the oven to 250 °C.

In a heavy-based saucepan, put 50 g butter with the little gems. Add salt and pepper, cover and cook over a low heat for 10–12 minutes.

Make the sauce. In a pan over a medium heat, sweat the shallots in 20 g butter until soft and translucent. Add the fish and chicken stock, wine, white-wine vinegar and parsley stalks and bring to the boil, reducing by three-quarters. Remove the parsley stalks and discard.

Put half the clarified butter in a large frying pan and fry the skate wings briefly on both sides, transferring them to an ovenproof dish in which all 4 wings will sit in a single layer. Pour the remaining butter over the skate and place in the oven for about 6 minutes.

Finish the sauce. Add a tablespoon of cream and then whisk in the last 20 g of diced butter.

Sieve before adding the capers and chopped parsley. Add lemon juice to taste.

To serve, cut the baby gems in half lengthways, arranging in the centre of the plate. Sit the skate wings on top and finish by spooning the sauce around and over the fish before garnishing with a little chopped parsley.

Sago with Coconut and Passion-fruit Sorbet

DESSERT Serves 6

200 g sago	passion-fruit sauce:
450 ml coconut milk	125 g passion-fruit purée
150 g sugar	125 g mango purée
1 vanilla pod	25 g sugar
½ mango	2 passion fruits
½ punnet strawberries	passion-fruit sorbet:
½ papaya	100 ml passion-fruit purée
½ small cantaloupe melon	sorbet syrup:
1 kiwi fruit	100 g caster sugar
¼ pineapple	60 g glucose
mint, to serve	150 ml water

Make the sauce. Bring the purées and sugar to the boil in a heavy-based pan. Strain. Add the passion-fruit seeds and refrigerate until needed.

Make the sorbet syrup. Put the caster sugar and glucose in a heavy-based pan with 150 ml water and boil for 1 minute, then cool to room temperature before refrigerating.

Make the sorbet. Mix together the passion-fruit purée and 100 ml of sorbet syrup and churn in an ice-cream machine until set. Freeze until needed in a plastic container with a lid.

Soak the sago in water for an hour. Drain and drop into boiling water, then cook until nearly translucent – about 3 minutes. Drain and wash under cold running water. Drain and refrigerate.

Boil the coconut milk and sugar with the vanilla pod. Strain and chill well.

Mix equal parts of the coconut cream and sago together and spoon into bowls. Slice the fruit and arrange around the sago. Serve with passion-fruit sorbet in the middle, drizzling with passion-fruit sauce. Garnish with a sprig of mint.

Above Even seasoned New Yorkers' jaws drop when they enter Guastavino's majestic space and appreciate the scale and beauty of what has so long remained hidden from them. Here we are looking down from the club balcony to the entrance and bar, with the restaurant to the left.
Opposite page: Left Ground plan of Guastavino's; **Right** The brasserie.

GUASTAVINO'S

When I look back over the last six years, I am astounded at how brave we were to take on this huge and daunting project – one that had previously defeated many an ambitious Manhattan entrepreneur. When I was first shown the derelict site under the 59th Street Bridge, my heart leapt. How could it be that this vast cathedral-like space, originally built as a farmers' market by the architect Rafael Guastavino in 1910, had been so long abandoned, used only as a storage place for street signs and as a home for tramps and wild dogs, while just across the street were the homes of the some of the richest people in the world?

Having decided to be brave, or foolhardy, we set about trying to gain permission to develop the site from the many community groups who – perhaps quite rightly – play such a vocal part in the development of Manhattan. Luckily the all-important Manhattan Landmarks was on our side as the site had been derelict for so long, and it had liked the many redevelopments that we had done in London.

The hard work then got underway, starting with a major excavation to create a huge basement for the Conran Shop. This, while separate from the restaurant, burrows underneath it and is entered by a chic little glass pavilion on the piazza we created outside. Guastavino's, with its restaurant, bars, club, private rooms and outdoor terrace, is at the east end of the site. Its soaring columns and domed ceilings are covered with the creamy ceramic tiles that are the signature of Rafael Guastavino's most innovative work, most notably found at Grand Central Station.

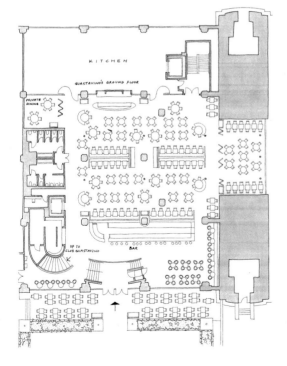

We planned a large buzzy brasserie for the ground floor with its own crustacea altar and open kitchen with a huge wood-fired oven. On top of this we built a mezzanine floor, which has become Club Guastavino, with its own bar and kitchen. At the front of the space is a large terrace facing flowerbeds and one of the few green lawns in Manhattan. And, as you enter, there is a huge bar, which has become one of Manhattan's favourite hangouts – no mean achievement in a city of hangouts.

Less than a year after we had opened, *Esquire* named us the 'best new restaurant in America', a welcome piece of recognition, especially after the enormous battle we had to open the place. Much of the praise should go to Daniel Orr, our extraordinarily energetic and talented executive chef whose kitchens produce outstandingly good food, both for the everyday brasserie and the smarter club. Joel Kissin used to oversee our restaurants in London but emigrated to America to be part of what is certainly our biggest and most complicated restaurant project to date.

Underneath the arches – Manhattan style

Above, left 59th Street Bridge – the site of Rafael Guastavino's magnificent Bridgemarket and now the restaurant complex named in his honour – soars away to Queens. On the piazza we built in front of Guastavino's is the horse trough that once stood inside the Bridgemarket. **Above,** The underside of the mezzanine above the brasserie is in cherrywood, slotted to improve the acoustics and absorb noise. **Below left** The arched entrance to the bar and restaurants.

Above Curved cherrywood banquettes subdivide the vast restaurant, creating a sense of warmth and intimacy in what might have been a vast and slightly chilly space. The simple but elegant aluminium chairs are designed by Vico Magistretti. **Right** The Conran Shop pavilion is in the piazza next to the restaurant. The main shop is in the basement, underneath Guastavino's. **Far right** The entrance staircase to Club Guastavino on the mezzanine.

A cathedral to the good life

Above A view from the club balcony showing the wonderful ceramic columns and vaults that we uncovered under the 59th Street Bridge.
Left As usual, we pay great attention to the design and quality of the bathrooms.
Opposite page: Top A view from the bar to the club balcony – the glass bar front can be lit with different colours; **Bottom left** A cheerful welcome at the reception desk; **Bottom right** The bar front reflected in the curved glass entrance screen.

Widely written about as one of the most stunning dining spaces in the world, Guastavino's has rapidly established itself as one of New York's most successful restaurants. The food is recognisably Conran, but also embraces American classics.

Recipes from Guastavino's

EXECUTIVE CHEF: Daniel Orr MANAGER: Chris Malm

Hot and Cold Pasta Salad with Rocket

STARTER Serves 4

8 ripe plum tomatoes
1 garlic clove,
　finely chopped
30 ml olive oil
1 tbsp thyme leaves
350 g linguini or
　spaghetti
30 ml basil-flavoured
　olive oil
2 tbsp lemon juice
2 bunches rocket
115 g Reggiano
　Parmigiano,
　shaved

Preheat the oven to 170 °C.

Cut the tomatoes in half and place cut-side up on a tray or roasting tin. Scatter over the garlic and thyme, dress with oil and season with salt and pepper. Roast for 35–45 minutes. Remove and reserve.

Bring a large pan of salted water to boil. Cook the pasta for 10 minutes. Drain then plunge immediately in cold water to stop further cooking. Drain and reserve.

In a sauté pan, warm the roasted tomatoes with a little olive oil and cook until golden. Finish the almost-cooked pasta by returning it to boiling salted water for 1 minute. Drain well, then toss in the pan with the tomatoes. Add the basil oil and season to taste with salt and freshly ground pepper.

Make a lemon vinaigrette by whisking together the olive oil and lemon juice, and use half of it to dress the pasta, giving it a final toss to distribute evenly.

Place the pasta on four warmed soup plates, with the tomatoes around the edge. In a bowl dress the rocket with the remaining dressing and arrange it over the pasta. Top with the shaved parmesan.

Halibut with Breadcrumbs, Tomato and Sherry Vinaigrette

MAIN Serves 4

4 halibut steaks
75 ml olive oil
1 lemon
1 small brown onion,
　thinly sliced
1 clove garlic, finely
　chopped
1 tbsp thyme leaves,
　chopped
1 fresh bay leaf
salt and pepper
1 cup herbed
　breadcrumbs
　(blitzed in a food
　processor with
　garlic, olive oil,
　thyme, rosemary,
　parsley leaves, salt
　and pepper)
vinaigrette:
25 ml extra-virgin
　olive oil
1 clove garlic,
　coarsely chopped
3 ripe plum
　tomatoes, peeled,
　seeded and
　chopped
15 Kalamata olives,
　pitted and roughly
　chopped
15 black olives,
　pitted and roughly
　chopped
15 salted capers,
　rinsed
1 salted anchovy
　fillet, rinsed and
　finely chopped
juice of ½ lemon
2 tbsp sherry vinegar
garnish: 8 sprigs
　curly parsley,
　deep-fried

Mix the olive oil, lemon, onion, garlic, thyme, bay leaf and pepper in a dish and rub the ingredients into the fish. Refrigerate for 4 hours.

Preheat the oven to 220 °C.

Remove the halibut from the marinade and top with the crumbs. Place a little of the marinade in a baking dish and lay the fish on top, not touching. Bake for 10 minutes.

In a small, heavy-based frying pan, fry the garlic in 1 tbsp olive oil until golden brown, then add the tomatoes. Mix in 8 thin lemon slices and onion, then the remaining vinaigrette ingredients.

Serve the halibut steaks over the vinaigrette. Garnish with deep-fried curly parsley.

Pastis Parfait with Candied Fennel and Blackberries

DESSERT Serves 8

170 g caster sugar
juice of half a lemon
8 egg yolks
75 ml pastis such as
　Pernod
575 ml double
　cream, whipped to
　form soft peaks,
　chilled well
500 g blackberries
　(for sauce and
　garnish)
candied fennel
fennel tops or mint
　for garnish

Spray a 20-cm spring-form pan with water and line with cling film. Chill in the freezer for 1 hour.

In a heavy-based pan, combine 115 g of the sugar with the lemon juice and 60 ml water and bring to a boil; then simmer and cook until it reaches 130 °C on a sugar thermometer. Remove the pan from the heat for 1 minute.

Whip the yolks until light and fluffy. Continuing to beat, add the hot syrup. Continue to beat until the mixture cools to room temperature. Add all but 2 tablespoons of the pastis, and a third of the whipped cream, and stir until incorporated. Gently fold in the remaining cream until it is thoroughly mixed. Pour the mixture into the spring-form pan. Freeze for at least 8 hours.

In a small saucepan, combine the remaining sugar with 3 tablespoons of water and boil. Remove from the heat, add two-thirds of the berries and blend. Pass through a sieve and finish with 2 tablespoons of pastis. Refrigerate until required.

To unmould the parfait, wrap a warm, moist tea towel around the mould to loosen it.

To serve, place the slices of the parfait on chilled plates and garnish with candied fennel, the blackberry sauce, the remaining whole blackberries and the fennel tops or mint.

Club Guastavino

Above The small 'velvet' private room at the top of the stairs in Club Guastavino. **Below, left to right:** Plan of the club; The curved stone staircase leading up to the club; Much of the service in the club is conducted from *guéridon* tables and trolleys. Visible is Tom Heatherwick's sculpture (*see* p. 128).

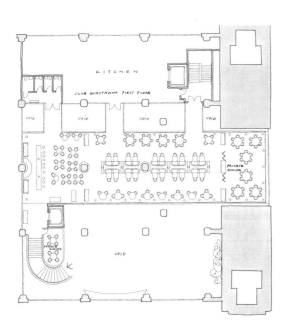

Above A view from the large private room in the club down the length of the restaurant. Below, left to right: The club bar table and stools; The waiters' stations have swivelling mirror screens that help create an atmosphere of reflected mystery and complement the whispering columns; The club bathrooms.

Recipes from Club Guastavino

EXECUTIVE CHEF: Daniel Orr MANAGER: Chris Malm

Chilled Golden Summer Soup

STARTER Serves 6

3 ears white
    sweetcorn
60 ml extra-virgin
    olive oil
2 cloves garlic,
    chopped
8–10 yellow
    tomatoes, roughly
    chopped
2 sweet onions,
    peeled and sliced
425 ml chicken stock
1 yellow pepper,
    de-seeded and
    diced
2 slices dried bread,
    diced
2 golden courgettes,
    cut in small dice

300 ml yellow pear
    tomatoes, halved
    (or substitute any
    vine-ripened
    tomato)
2 beefsteak
    tomatoes, diced
½ tsp chilli sauce
¼ tsp five-spice
    powder
1 tsp lemon zest
¼ bunch chives,
    chopped
handful picked
    coriander, coarsely
    chopped
salt

Bring a pan of salted water to boil. Cut the corn from the cobs and blanch for 1 minute. Drain and reserve.

In a large pan heat the oil until very hot and throw in the garlic. Stirring continuously, allow to brown lightly, then quickly add the tomatoes, onions, chicken stock, half the yellow pepper and the bread. Bring to a boil, reduce to a simmer and cook for 15–20 minutes or until tender. Purée in a food processor, pass through a fine sieve into a bowl and chill. Leave to cool before adding the remaining pepper, corn, courgettes, tomatoes, and herbs. Taste and adjust the seasoning.

Mound on cold soup plates and serve.

Quail Stuffed with Black Pudding, Dates and Pinenuts

MAIN Serves 6

400 g black pudding
1 tsp olive oil
6 shallots, peeled
    and chopped
1 garlic clove, peeled
    and finely chopped
1 tbsp pinenuts,
    toasted
3 dates, pitted and
    diced
1 tsp fresh thyme,
    chopped

6 boneless quail
6 rosemary twigs
30 g butter, softened
3 sprigs thyme
60-ml cup white wine
60-ml cup chicken
    stock
1 tbsp sherry vinegar
18 pickling onions,
    peeled

Remove the skin from the black pudding and mash with a fork.

Put the olive oil in a small pan over a medium heat and sweat the shallots until soft and translucent. Add the garlic and toss, then cool and refrigerate for an hour. Mix together the shallots, pinenuts, dates, spices and thyme, seasoning with salt and pepper to taste.

Preheat the oven to 250 °C.

Lay the quails breast-side down and season with salt and pepper and a little garlic. Fill with the stuffing. Close each quail with a rosemary skewer and rub with butter. Season again with salt and freshly ground black pepper.

Place a sprig of thyme in three small baking dishes, putting two quails – breast upwards – on top of each. Add the wine, chicken stock, vinegar and onions, and bake for 10 minutes, or until the birds are brown and crisp on the outside and just cooked through.

Leave to rest for 5 minutes in a warm place before serving.

Spiced Tarte Tatin with Honey and Ginger

DESSERT Serves 6

225 ml honey
10 Granny Smith
    apples, peeled and
    quartered
spice mix:
¼ tsp each of ground
    cloves, cardamom,
    cinnamon and
    nutmeg
3-cm piece ginger,
    peeled and finely
    chopped
½ tsp lemon zest

50 g butter
pinch of salt
500 g butter puff
    pastry
60 g caster sugar
1 tbsp calvados
225 ml warm caramel
    sauce (see p. 137)
2 tbsp raisins,
    soaked in calvados
    for 24 hours

Preheat the oven to 220 °C.

Heat a large non-stick ovenproof pan over a high heat and pour in the honey. Allow it to caramelize, then add the apples. Cook the apples, turning frequently until they are browned all over and start to soften. Add the spices, ginger, lemon, butter and salt, and mix well. Leave to cool to room temperature, then refrigerate for 2 hours.

Roll out the pastry to a thickness of 1 cm. Tear into pieces and cover the apples with them. Scatter a little sugar on top and bake for 20 to 25 minutes when the pastry will be well risen and have taken a golden colour. If the pastry shows signs of burning before it is cooked through, cover lightly with foil.

Remove and rest for 3–4 minutes before turning out onto a board. Push the apples together and sprinkle with calvados. Mix the raisins and caramel, and spoon over the tart.

Serve warm with crème fraîche or ice cream and a final drizzle of caramel sauce.

The club's quiet distinction contrasts with the bustling larger-scale main restaurant. The food is always elegant and simple.

Down to the smallest detail...

Opposite page Tom Heatherwick's beautiful golden sculpture appears to ripple out of the gaps between the giant granite slabs that support the bridge. **Above, left** The specially designed zinc ashtrays for American cigar smokers. **Above** Beautiful vases – flowers are an integral part of all our restaurants. **Top** Pinch pots for sea salt and cracked pepper. **Right** An insulated wine bucket made out of aluminium, blue steel and nickel.

Left The spectacular double-height space of the Mezzo complex, with a view of Mezzonine on the ground floor and the Mezzo restaurant in the basement. The two-level kitchens are on the right.
Opposite page:
Left Plan of the basement complex;
Right The entrance to Mezzo on Soho's Wardour Street.

When Mezzo first opened on the site of the old Marquee Club some six years ago, I wrote:

'I want Mezzo to make people feel good, to…bring something quite new to Soho. Mezzo is jolly and stylish, and although it's big it's not conceived as one huge space, but as a series of independent but complementary projects in a large air-conditioned envelope.

'I hope Mezzo gives people such a thrill and excitement that their jaws drop when they see it for the first time: the enormous open void between Mezzonine upstairs and the Mezzo restaurant downstairs; the dramatic, curvaceous staircase; the theatre of the opened-up kitchens; the specially commissioned artwork. Wow!

'Mezzo is definitely the most exciting but also the most difficult project we've done to date, turning a derelict site into a fantastic restaurant. A lot of money has been spent on technology the public will never notice. No one has ever done anything like this before…

'Ultimately, the people and the food are what will count. There will be a very different emphasis between upstairs – which is bright, modern and simple, with fresh, clean, unusual Asian flavours in the cooking – and downstairs – where the furnishing is more colourful and the menu more classically inspired. Different venues for different occasions for all sorts of different people.'

Since then we have fed and entertained several million people, and Mezzo – its bars, café, and restaurant – has undoubtedly been the major entertainment venue in London's vibrant Soho. Building a space like Mezzo and Mezzonine, with its two large kitchens and

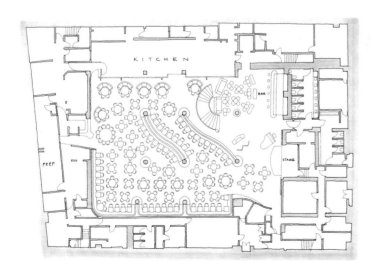

huge infrastructure of staff facilities, storage and preparation, is very complex, and the fact that it has performed well over the years says a lot about its planning, design and construction. Of course, there have been some changes but the basic infrastructure remains intact. Chefs also change. David Laris, our present executive chef, brings with him years of experience in Australia and the Far East and produces food that is stylish and at times unusual but always delicious.

The music, too, has evolved: a DJ plays in the upstairs bar at night, while there's live music most nights of the week downstairs. The Mezzo Café has been transmogrified in a rather Moroccan way, serving kebabs, and Greek hummus and taramasalata. That's the great thing about the restaurant business – it never stays still, new ideas are always percolating upwards and outwards. Nothing ventured, nothing gained.

The Mezzo restaurant: an elegant space in crowded Soho

Above, left The vibrantly busy Mezzo dining area reflected in the faceted double-height mirrors. **Above, right** The glamorous Mezzo reception, with a view over part of the restaurant reflected in angled mirrors over the banquette seats, with Allen Jones's talking heads below. **Opposite page: Main picture** The Mezzo restaurant's curved entrance staircase and glazed bridge. However lively the restaurant becomes, the effect is always one of elegant spaciousness; **Far right, top** Another recent addition to Mezzo – the private room; **Far right, bottom** The well-designed lavatories have to be durable since they are used by hundreds of people every day.

Mezzo at night

Above Lighting plays an important part in changing day into night. **Below, left** Fresh flowers are important in all our restaurants. **Below, right** Allen Jones's vibrant painted screen conveys something of Mezzo's joyous atmosphere. At night it slides back to reveal the stage.

Above Cocktails by the piano: a sophisticated evening in the handsome Mezzoluna Bar. Below Live music occurs on most nights at Mezzo. Below, right The Mezzoluna Bar viewed from the curved entrance stair: ideal for making that glamorous entrance.

The best
contemporary
cooking draws on
a global larder.
Mezzo offers vivid
flavours and stylish
presentation.
Following pages:
The intense energy
of food preparation
in Mezzo's huge,
open kitchens.

Recipes from Mezzo

EXECUTIVE CHEF/MANAGER: David Laris

Feta cheese, Cracked Wheat, Oregano and Parsley Salad

STARTER Serves 6

sourdough bread	150 g cracked wheat,
200 g rocket leaves	soaked
400 g feta cheese	**vinaigrette:**
5 ripe tomatoes,	2 tsp red-wine
chopped	vinegar
handful flat-leaf	30 ml olive oil
parsley	salt and pepper

Make a vinaigrette with the vinegar, olive oil, salt and pepper. Reserve.

Cut 6 thin slices of bread and toast lightly.

In a bowl toss the rocket with the vinaigrette to coat evenly. Distribute the rocket between four large plates, mounding in the centre. Mix all other ingredients and place on the rocket leaves, finishing with a slice of toasted sourdough.

Pan-fried Red Mullet, with Chorizo and Paprika Oil

MAIN Serves 4

400 g mild chorizo	handful of chervil
200 g baby fennel	salt
8 x 100 to 115-g red	**paprika oil:**
mullet fillets, skin	75 g garlic, peeled
on and pin-boned	and chopped
dash of oil	75 g shallots, peeled
16 Kalamata olives	and chopped
1 tbsp pickled	500 ml olive oil
lemons	50 g paprika

Make the paprika oil. Over a low heat and in a heavy-based pan, sweat the garlic and shallots in 4 tbsp of the oil until soft and translucent. Add the paprika and stir vigorously with a wooden spoon, continuing to fry for a couple of minutes to cook the raw taste from the spice.

Add the rest of the oil and leave over the lowest heat for 15 minutes, then pass through a sieve lined with butter muslin. This will keep in the fridge in a sealed container for 4 weeks.

Preheat a ridged grill-pan until smoking hot. Slice the chorizo lengthways and lay it cut-side downwards at a 45-degrees angle to the ridges. Sear for 2 minutes. Remove and keep warm.

Bring a pan of lightly salted water to boil. Cook the fennel until tender – about 5 minutes.

Preheat a heavy-based frying pan until very hot. Brush the mullet fillets on both sides with oil and season with salt and pepper. Lay in the pan, flesh-side down, for 1 minute. Turn and cook for a further minute. Remove to a warm plate.

Warm the chorizo, fennel and olives in a little paprika oil and layer on flat plates interleaving fish, sausage and fennel. Spoon paprika oil around the dish and garnish with pickled lemon and sprigs of chervil.

Sticky Date Pudding with Whisky Caramel Sauce and Crème Anglaise

DESSERT Serves 6–8

350 g dried dates	8 egg yolks
2 tsp bicarbonate of	100 g caster sugar
soda	**whisky caramel**
100 g unsalted butter	**sauce:**
350 g sugar	300 g caster sugar
4 eggs	400 ml double cream
350 g plain flour	40 ml whisky
1 tsp baking powder	150 g chilled
crème anglaise:	unsalted butter,
500 ml full-fat milk	diced
2 vanilla pods, split	

Bring the dates to boil in 600 ml water. Simmer until the dates have plumped up and are soft – about 20–30 minutes – when almost all the water will have been absorbed by the dates or evaporated. Stir in the bicarbonate of soda, remove from the heat and leave to cool.

Preheat the oven to 190 °C.

Cream the butter and sugar until light and fluffy, then, one at a time, whisk in the eggs. Mix in the flour and baking powder, then add the date mixture and beat together to mix evenly with a wooden spoon.

Spoon into 300-ml dariole moulds or ramekins and sit them in an ovenproof dish or roasting tin, not touching. Put in the oven then pour very hot water into the tin to come halfway up the moulds. Cook for 50 minutes.

Make the crème anglaise. Put the milk in a pan and add the split vanilla pods and seeds. Bring slowly to the boil.

Whisk the yolks and sugar until pale. Slowly whisk in the milk and return to a clean saucepan. Simmer, stirring constantly, until the sauce thickens to a custard. Pour through a fine sieve and leave to cool. Reheat gently before serving.

Make the whisky caramel sauce. Put the sugar and 100 ml cold water into a small, heavy-based saucepan and bring to a boil. Lower the heat and take to 180 °C on a sugar thermometer. At this point the caramel will have coloured from a light blond to a dark golden brown.

Remove the pan from the heat and gradually whisk in the cream. Start with a spoonful at a time as the mixture will rise dangerously when the cold cream hits the very hot toffee. When all the cream has been amalgamated, gradually stir in the whisky and then the butter dice until incorporated into a smooth creamy sauce. Return to the boil briefly and remove from the heat.

To serve, turn out the puddings from the moulds into warmed bowls. Drizzle the puddings with the toffee sauce and pour the crème anglaise around.

The Mezzonine bar and restaurant

Opposite page: **Main picture** The beautiful cool-grey entrance bar under the glass skylight makes a wonderful place to relax and drink; **Bottom, left** The striking glass entrance screen, with the skylight above and the bar behind; **Bottom, right** The ground-floor reception with the Mezzonine bar curving away into the background. The emphasis here is on the creation of a well-defined, harmonious, and welcoming space.

This page: **Top left** The Mezzonine restaurant: the subtle use of lighting can create a warm, intimate space even in quite a large area. The restaurant walls are decorated with a photographic reportage of Soho life; **Top right** The mosaic front of the bar; **Right** The private room is screened from the restaurant by a curved pierced screen, which holds an eclectic array of objects, from vases to musical instruments; **Below** Plan of the Mezzonine and entrance; **Bottom, right** The bar has its own DJ booth.

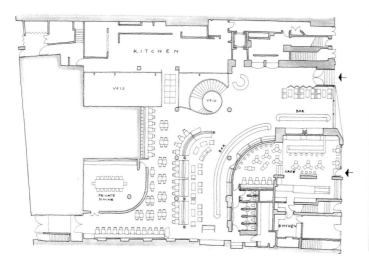

Recipes from Mezzonine

EXECUTIVE CHEF/MANAGER: David Laris

Seared Tuna, Asian Marinade, and Bean Sprouts

STARTER Serves 4

75 ml vegetable oil	400 g very fresh tuna
½ tsp turmeric	loin, trimmed of
6 shallots, peeled	skin and blood
and sliced	marks
paper-thin	4 spring onions
2 garlic cloves,	120 g bean sprouts
peeled and sliced	handful of Thai basil
paper-thin	handful of mint
1 tbsp coriander	20 g sugar
seeds	20 ml rice vinegar
1 tbsp Szechwan	2 hot red chillies,
pepper	shredded
	2 tsp fish sauce

Put 3 tablespoons of vegetable oil in a small pan over a low heat. Add the turmeric and stir in. Leave over the lowest heat for 2 minutes. With a wooden spoon, push through a muslin-lined sieve into a jug and reserve.

Put the remaining oil in a frying pan over a low heat and add the shallots. Sweat, stirring frequently, until softened and translucent. Add the garlic, stir in and cook for 2 minutes. Turn up the heat to medium and – stirring continuously – continue frying until golden and crisp. Remove onto kitchen paper to drain and reserve.

Coarsely crush the coriander and Szechwan pepper by putting them in a plastic bag and rolling with a heavy rolling pin. Transfer to a tray or Swiss roll tin. Brush the tuna with a little oil and then roll to coat evenly with the spices.

Put a heavy-based frying pan over a high heat, and, when it is smoking hot, sear the tuna briefly on all sides, giving each plane about 15 seconds. Immediately transfer to a bowl of iced water to stop further cooking. Remove and pat dry with kitchen paper then wrap tightly in cling film and refrigerate until needed. It can be cooked and held like this for up to 4 hours.

Unwrap the tuna and cut into 2-cm slices with a razor-sharp knife. Cut the spring onions on the bias in 2-cm pieces.

In a bowl mix the bean sprouts with the herbs, crispy-fried shallots and garlic, the spring onions, sugar, rice vinegar, chilli and fish sauce.

To serve, mound the salad on large white plates, arrange the tuna on top and drizzle with the turmeric oil to finish.

Stir-fried Prawns and Scallops with Asian Greens

MAIN Serves 4

100 ml vegetable oil	small bunch of
4 garlic cloves,	coriander
peeled and	50 ml soy sauce
chopped	50 ml fish sauce
2.5-cm piece of	50 g caster sugar
ginger, peeled and	small bunch of Thai
chopped	basil
1 kg king prawns	100 ml oyster sauce
8 scallops	500 g bok choi (if not
2 hot red chillies,	available, broccoli
shredded	is fine)
	200 g bean sprouts

Heat a wok or large non-stick frying pan and add the vegetable oil. When the oil is smoking hot, add the garlic, ginger, prawns and scallops, stir-frying briefly until the prawns and scallops are just cooked – about 1 minute.

Add the chilli, coriander, soy sauce, fish sauce, sugar, Thai basil, oyster sauce and a dash of water, then combine with a couple of good stirs. Add the bok choi and bean sprouts and continue to cook for 2 minutes.

Serve in large bowls with steamed rice, offering a garnish of sliced chilli and coriander leaves separately.

Pavlova with Fresh Berries

DESSERT Serves 4

pavlovas:	coulis:
6 egg whites	1 punnet strawberries
200 g sugar	1 punnet raspberries
1 tsp vanilla essence	1 punnet blueberries
1 tsp white-wine or	1 punnet blackberries
champagne	200 g caster sugar
vinegar	
40 ml boiling water	200 ml double cream
	icing sugar, to dust

In a bowl of an electric mixer fitted with a balloon whisk, whisk the egg whites and sugar at full speed for 1 minute. Put the vanilla and vinegar in 40 ml of boiling water. Add to the egg white gradually and continue to whisk for a further 9 minutes.

Preheat the oven to 140 °C.

With a large spoon, spread the mixture in 4 mounded circles on a silicone baking sheet or on greaseproof paper on a baking sheet.

Bake for 55–60 minutes. The pavlovas should be crisp but only lightly tinted on the outside and marshmallow-soft in the centre.

Reserve a few whole berries. Put the rest in a pan with the sugar, bring to the boil and liquidize. Sieve and cool. Stir a few of the whole berries.

Whisk the cream until thick enough to scoop.

To serve, put a pavlova in the centre of each plate. Spoon cream into the well and top with coulis, allowing some to overflow at one point. Garnish with the whole berries and dust lightly with icing sugar.

Mezzonine is an informal bar and dining area on the ground floor, where the food is largely Asian and Far Eastern in its influences.

Mezzo Café: while away an evening in Soho

Above, left to right: The Mezzo Café makes a very easy and informal atmosphere for a coffee, a beer, or a plate of tasty Middle Eastern food; A view into the café and grill; Mezzo was once the site of the Marquee Club – many of the names of the famous musicians who played there are stamped into the lead front of the café; Chargrilled kebabs and the Mezzo Café sign; A display behind the bar – cigarettes are always in demand. **Below, left** The handsome entrance door, reminiscent of art deco. **Right** The attractive, welcoming frontage to the café. **Far right** A simple counter for a quick cappuccino.

JOE COCKER   BLACK SABBATH   LED ZEPPELIN   DEEP PUR

INXS   KIKI DEE   JUDAS PRIEST   CRIS ISAAK   THOMPSON

ON BLUE   DIRE STRAITS   TERENCE TRENT D'ARBY   AC/DC

THE PRETENDERS   HUMAN LEAGUE   SIMPLE MINDS   IRON M

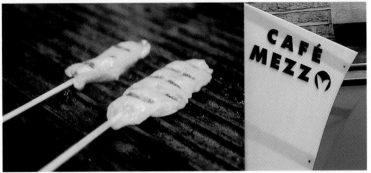

CAFÉ
MEZZO

Left The gardens
of St Marylebone's
Church reflected in
the mirrors at the
back of Orrery.
Opposite page:
Left Plan of the
restaurant; Right
Elegant Orrery menus.

ORRERY

We had been looking for a site for a second Conran Shop, north of Hyde Park for some time. The moment I saw the estate agent's particulars for 55 Marylebone High Street – a derelict stables building opposite the enchanting St Marylebone Church – I knew it was the place.

The Howard de Walden Estate, who own most of the land in the area, realized that a new building with a Conran Shop and restaurant would send out a powerful signal about the revitalization of the High Street, which had become very down-at-heel, so we were able to lease the site at a very reasonable ground rent. Conran & Partners designed a simple but elegant building, retaining only the façade of the old stables, and made a beautiful space for a restaurant on the first floor, overlooking the church gardens. The excellent self-contained kitchen is on the ground and first floors, reached by crossing the top of the arch that divides the two buildings.

The restaurant itself is a long narrow room with windows fitted with portholes down one side and banquettes divided with 'confessional' screens in sycamore down the other. Mirrors reflect the leafy church garden outside. The curved ceiling is punctuated by roof lights, which provide a wonderful quality of natural light and ventilation as well as a view onto the terrace above – used for pre-dinner drinks in summer.

In the entrance hall is a beautiful orrery, which is on loan from the National Maritime Museum at Greenwich. I have always been fascinated by these astrological devices, used for plotting the annual motion of the earth in relation to the sun and moon and the planets. The restaurant's main decoration, though, is inspired by the work of Italian still-life painter Giorgio Morandi. A long shelf runs the entire length of the restaurant, on which there are subtle arrangements of pots, jugs, carafes, bowls and bottles that reflect those found in Morandi's work. There's also a small comfortable bar furnished with velour-covered upholstered chairs and sofas, designed by Josef Hoffmann for the Wiener Werkstätte.

This is a starred restaurant, which reflects the quality and style of food, the service, the wine list and the outstanding cheese trolley. The head chef, Chris Galvin, and his kitchen produce food of a remarkably high standard from the freshest and finest ingredients available – Pyrenean milk-fed lamb, line-caught Cornish sea bass, diver-caught scallops, Scottish lobsters and grouse, truffles from Périgord and Alba and so on. Everything is seasonal and at its best. Patrick Fischnaller manages the restaurant, and it runs like a well-oiled orrery, much to the delight of its classy customers.

Top, left to right: Arched windows, each with a central porthole, overlook St Marylebone churchyard; A broad view down the length of the restaurant; Sycamore 'confessional' screens divide the banquettes; Orrery prides itself on its fine selection of wines and liqueurs; The Orrery on loan from the

National Maritime Museum in the entrance hall. **Bottom, left to right:** Hoffmann furniture in the bar; On warm sunny days the terrace above the restaurant is used for drinks and coffee; Bottles, carafes, bowls and boxes, Morandi-style; The generous cheese selection; The fine Orrery humidor.

As you would expect in a Michelin-starred restaurant, the food is essentially French and the service polished and professional. This is a special place to eat. **Previous pages:** The finest raw materials are used in Orrery's food.

Recipes from Orrery

CHEF: Chris Galvin MANAGER: Patrick Fischnaller

Lobster Bisque

STARTER Serves 4–6 people

150 ml olive oil	2 tbsp whipping
2 x 750-g lobsters	cream
2 tbsp tomato purée	50 g butter
100 ml brandy	**mirepoix:**
200 ml white wine	50 g onion, chopped
6 parsley stalks	50 g carrot, chopped
1 bay leaf	50 g fennel, chopped
1 sprig thyme	50 g leek, chopped
1.5 litre chicken	
stock	
cayenne pepper	

Heat the olive oil in a thick-bottomed pan. Cut the lobsters' tails into 3 sections and cut the claws off. Drop the lobster pieces into the pan and toss until it takes on a good red colour. Remove from the heat, pick the meat out, then chop and reserve for the garnish.

Use a cutlet bat or the back of a heavy cleaver to smash the shells into small pieces.

Put the same pan over a medium heat with the oil and add the mirepoix and tomato purée. Fry until the vegetables have taken a good colour, then add the shell pieces followed by the brandy and wine. Reduce by half at a fast boil. Add the parsley stalk, bay and thyme. Add the stock and rice, then lower the heat to simmer. Cook for 45 minutes, skimming the surface frequently.

Remove and leave until cool enough to handle, and then put through a mouli or purée in a food processor. Pass through a sieve. Taste, adjust the seasoning and sprinkle in a little cayenne. In a small pan bring the cream to a boil and then whisk it and the butter into the bisque.

Serve in warmed bowls, dividing the lobster meat equally between them.

Roast Squab Pigeon, Petit Pois and Girolles

MAIN Serves 4

4 x 400 to 450-g	½ tbsp crème fraîche
squab pigeons	1 ½ tbsp golden
120 g butter	chicken stock
salt and pepper	1 tbsp dried
12 button onions	gingerbread
24 x 3 x 1 cm	crumbs, fried
streaky-bacon	golden in butter
lardons	½ tbsp chopped
120 g girolles	parsley
200 g petit pois	

Preheat the oven to 180 °C.

Rub the birds in butter, put in a roasting tin and season generously with salt and pepper. Roast on one side for 2 minutes, then turn and roast for another 2 minutes. Baste with the foaming butter from the tin and cook for a further 7 minutes. Remove from the pan and rest in a warm place for 10 minutes.

Add a knob of butter to the roasting tin over a low-to-medium heat and gently colour the button onions. Add the lardons and fry until they colour, and then add the girolles, tossing all together to evaporate any excess moisture.

Drain any fat from the pan and add the petit pois. Shake together and add a little crème fraîche and chicken stock, then allow to bubble and emulsify before checking the seasoning.

Sprinkle the pigeon with the gingerbread crumbs and return to the oven for 30 seconds. Remove and carve off the legs, cutting through the joints into drumsticks and thighs. Remove the breasts whole and slice on the bias into four or five pieces.

To serve, spoon the petit pois and girolles onto warmed plates, arranging the pigeon on top, and sprinkle with parsley.

Vanilla and Yogurt Bavarois with Rose-water Syrup, Grilled Figs and Pistachios

DESSERT Makes 10 x 150-ml moulds

325 ml double cream	**syrup:**
1 vanilla pod	500 ml water
½ tsp orange zest	250 g sugar
150 g caster sugar	50 ml rose water
10 g gelatin	fresh figs (5 halves
175 ml whipping	per portion)
cream	icing sugar for
600 ml Greek yogurt	dusting
	10 g pistachios,
	blanched

Make the bavarois. Put 150 ml of the double cream in a pan, add the vanilla pod, orange zest and caster sugar, and bring to the boil. Remove from heat. Stir in the gelatin and leave to cool.

Whisk 175 ml of double cream together with the whipping cream until lightly whipped, and set aside.

Fold the Greek yogurt into the cooled mixture, then carefully fold in the whipped cream. Pour the mixture into individual dariole moulds or ramekins, cover with cling film and leave to set in the fridge or at least 4 hours.

Make the syrup. Heat 500 ml water in a pan, dissolve the sugar and stir in the rose water.

Preheat the grill. Slice the figs in half lengthways, put them face up on a baking tray and dust liberally with icing sugar. Grill the figs until they become juicy and start to colour.

To serve, remove the bavarois from the fridge, dip each mould in hot water for about 10 seconds, then invert, intact, onto the serving plate. Arrange five grilled fig halves around the bavarois, spoon the rose-water syrup over and around the figs and sprinkle with pistachios. Serve immediately.

Left Le Pont de la Tour's imposing double-height entrance. To the left is the crustacea counter, with its Pompeii-like mosaic and Tom Dixon's wonderful fishy chandelier.
Opposite page:
Left Plan of the restaurant; **Right** A matchbox featuring the restaurant's logo, which, not surprisingly, is Tower Bridge.

LE PONT DE LA TOUR

The heart of our Butlers Wharf Gastrodrome, Le Pont de la Tour first opened in September 1991. Stretching 150 feet along the Thames riverside, it comprises a grill and bar and a large restaurant, both with outside seating; a private room; a large wine merchants with a stock of some 7,000 bottles in its cellars; a small specialist food store; a bakery; and a coffee kiosk selling croissants and pâtisserie. This group of gastronomic ventures formed the real nucleus of our development of the derelict Butlers Wharf.

The 'Pont' really was the bridge that caused City people to cross the river. Its star attraction, of course, is the sheer quality of its generous, simple food – the piles of lobsters, langoustines, oysters and clams served from the grand crustacea counter, and the gorgeous *plateaux de fruits de mer* and large plates of *steak frites* served from the bar. Important to the design are Tom Dixon's enormous fishy chandelier and Patrick Cauldfield's etched-glass screens and lead panels indented with fish scales.

In the summer the bar and grill bursts out onto the waterfront under a pale cream canopy. A huge pig trough filled with flowers and greenery runs the full length of the restaurant and protects customers from the bustle of the busy riverside walk. The restaurant itself is much calmer. As you hand in your coat at the reception, you can look into the kitchen and see flames leaping from the enormous grill. You are then greeted by a display of seasonal produce on a large marble slab and by the view down the long narrow restaurant. Sash windows open onto the river, their white voile curtains fluttering in the breeze. Outdoor seating is on one side, and a wall decorated by Sem's drawings of French society misbehaving, circa 1900, is on the other. The restaurant is reminiscent of the dining room of a 1930s liner, and the chairs were in fact inspired by the

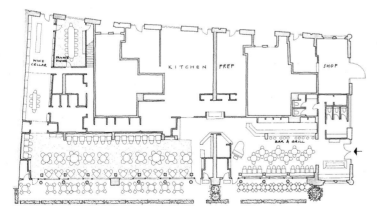

Normandie's second-class dining-room furniture. When the river is high and a boat passes, you feel that you, too, are out on the water. The wine cellar-cum-merchant is attached to the restaurant at the far end, and its contribution is reflected in the very fine wine list.

The quality of the food, the professional service, the buzzy grill and bar, and the spectacular views encompassing Tower Bridge and the Tower of London all help to make Le Pont de la Tour one of London's most popular restaurants. No wonder, then, that this was the restaurant that Tony and Cherie Blair took Bill and Hilary Clinton to for a family outing.

The heart of the Thames-side Gastrodrome

Top left The outdoor seating with river views becomes very popular once the weather turns warm and sunny. **Above, far left** A very large cream canopy covers the outside seating and waiters' stations. **Above, left** The reception desk with the Bibendum cigar humidor behind. **Above** A view down the length of the restaurant with the Sem drawings on the back wall. **Opposite page: Top left** The entrance to the restaurant with a display of raw vegetables and a chilled cheese safe; **Top right** Classic details; **Bottom left** The central waiters' station with a miniature model of Le Pont de la Tour on top; **Bottom right** The private room has a wall of wine down one side.

Recipes from Le Pont de la Tour

CHEF: Tim Powell MANAGER: Robert MacDonald

Veal Sweetbreads with Morels and Broad Beans

STARTER Serves 4

2 tbsp vegetable oil
30 g butter
600 g veal sweetbreads,
2 garlic cloves, finely chopped
85 g morels
200 ml double cream

120 g broad beans, blanched
2 tbsp flat-leaf parsley, chopped
4 thick slices of brioche
salt and pepper

Heat the oil and butter in a heavy-based frying pan over a medium heat until the butter foams. Season the sweetbreads and brown for 2 minutes on both sides. Remove from the pan and rest in a warm place.

Turn down the heat, add the garlic and sweat until soft. Add the morels, turn up the heat a little and fry for about 2 minutes. Add the cream, broad beans and parsley. Bring to the boil, then remove and season to taste.

Slice the sweetbreads in three and lay on top of the brioche. Arrange on warmed plates, spooning the sauce over. Serve immediately.

Poached Lobster with Herb Butter Sauce

MAIN Serves 4

coarse sea salt
4 x 600/700-g live lobsters (preferably native, but Canadian will do)

butter sauce:
2 shallots, roughly chopped
2 bay leaves
200 ml vermouth or dry white wine
200 ml double cream
250 g salted butter

ground paprika
juice of 1 lemon
herbs, all roughly chopped:
handful flat-leaf parsley

handful of chives
handful of dill
handful of chervil
handful of tarragon

Bring a large pot of water, seasoned with coarse sea salt, to the boil. You need lots of salt, about 140 g salt to every 5 litres of water. This will give you a salinity equivalent to that of the sea. Boil the lobsters. Lobsters this size will take around 14–15 minutes.

While the lobsters are cooking, in a small pan bring the vermouth to the boil with the shallots and bay leaves and reduce by half. Add the double cream, return to the boil and immediately remove from the heat. Pass through a sieve into another pan.

Reheat and whisk in the butter, seasoning with paprika to taste. Add the lemon juice and roughly chopped herbs.

When the lobsters are cooked, cut in half lengthways with a large chef's knife. If you are right-handed, put the lobster on its belly and with the head pointing to the right. Position the point of the knife or leading edge of the cleaver centrally at the point where the head joins the tail section, then drive down and cut through the head, slamming down with the flat of your hand on the knife to cut cleanly through the shell.

Turn the lobster, reinsert the knife in the same central line and cut through to the tail, separating it into two halves. Crack the claws to release the meat, pour over sauce and serve immediately with boiled Jersey Royals and a green salad.

Dark-chocolate Mousse with Hazelnut Meringue

DESSERT Serves 4

meringue:
75 g hazelnuts, shelled, roasted and skinned
35 g plain flour
3 large eggs
110 g caster sugar
60 g unsalted melted butter

mousse:
250 g dark chocolate
60 g unsalted butter
135 g egg yolk
165 g egg white
10 g caster sugar

Make the meringue. Preheat the oven to 120 °C. Line 3 oven trays with lightly oiled baking paper.

Put the hazelnuts into a food processor and process to a granular consistency, then add the flour. Beat the egg whites with half the sugar until soft, then add the hazelnut flour with the remaining sugar. Fold in the melted butter.

Divide the mixture between the trays, spreading with a palette knife to approximately 1-cm thick. Put the trays in the oven and bake for about 45 minutes, when the meringues will be crisp. Remove from the oven and immediately turn out and remove the baking paper. Leave to cool on a wire rack.

Make the chocolate mousse. Melt the chocolate in a bowl over simmering water. Then add the butter. Remove from heat and add the egg yolk, stirring all the time.

With a mixer, beat the egg white and sugar to create a meringue texture. Stir 1 tbsp into the melted chocolate and butter, then fold in the rest carefully. Cover and place in fridge to set.

Approximately 3 hours before you serve, layer the meringue and chocolate mousse, finishing with a layer of chocolate mousse. Serve with fresh raspberries and crème fraîche.

Classic French dishes sit happily on a menu that also features the freshest crustacea and seafood. Le Pont de la Tour is also renowned for its wine list.

Le Pont de la Tour's bar

This page: Top left: The corridor to the lavatories – the wavy handles refer to the nearby river. **Far left, centre** Fish scales by Patrick Cauldfield are indented into the lead on the front of the restaurant. **Left, centre** Piano music every night in the bar. **Far left, bottom** Outdoor seating for the bar. **Left, bottom** Patrick Cauldfield's etched-glass fish. **Below** Specially designed chairs and tables. **Opposite page: Main picture** The bar front is covered with pressed aluminium – the pattern reminds me of shoals of tiny fish, Note, too, the shelf supports, which take the form of carved, blue-stained fish. The bar stools are our own design; **Right, top to bottom** The crustacea counter with its underwater mosaic and copper lobsters made by Tom Dixon; A busy lunchtime.

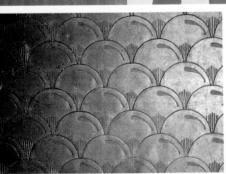

The Gastrodrome bakery and shops

Top, left to right The jazzy coffee kiosk at Butlers Wharf Gastrodrome; The Food Store; The well-stocked wine merchants, which also serves as the restaurant's wine cellar as well as having its own off-licence sales; The Pont

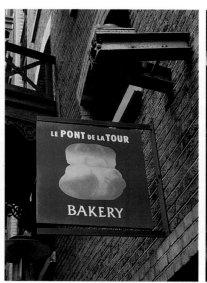

shop is what every neighbourhood deli should be – an Aladdin's cave of tempting goodies and fresh seasonal produce; **Bottom, left to right** The Pont bakery is a very important part of the Gastrodrome. Its excellent breads are served in all the restaurants and are also for sale in the shop.

Above A view through the etched glass screens down the length of the restaurant towards the Mezzanine bar – a huge glass skylight runs down the centre of the restaurant. **Opposite page: Left** Plan of the restaurant; **Right** The classic 'Q' ashtray.

QUAGLINO'S

I'm very proud of Quaglino's. When the restaurant opened on Valentine's Day, 1993, I wrote:

'Quaglino's was a very dazzling restaurant in the 1930s and had a particular place in the social history of those times. In this second incarnation I hope it will become the most spectacular restaurant of the 1990s, bringing glamour to the rather different social life of modern London.

'I have always believed that there was room in London for an equivalent of the great Parisian brasseries, or perhaps something a little better, where the buzz of the room was matched by excellent food and wine. The new Quag's is designed to be a huge, bustling place of entertainment, in the spirit of the last decade of the Millennium.

'Many of the qualities that made the original Quaglino's a great restaurant are being carefully revived. John Quaglino was evidently someone who loved food and believed its enjoyment was a vital part of civilized life. I am a man after his own heart. His restaurant was a place of pleasure, where music, dancing and wine gave a sense of well-being. Although the dress code and the celestial prices have gone, a similar spirit will prevail.

'So many people celebrated great days in their lives with a meal at Quaglino's, and everyone involved with the project has been struck by the warmth with which Quag's is remembered. Our ambition is to re-create that wonderful sense of occasion, in a style suited to the end of the century.

'This new Quaglino's is designed as an entirely modern restaurant of glamour and entertainment, where the food and service will reflect the achievement of London, which in the last few years has become the gastronomic centre of the world.'

Nearly nine years later, I think it's reasonable to say that we have achieved my ambition. Today the restaurant is virtually unchanged from the day we first opened, although there is continual refurbishment and maintenance, with the replacement of exhausted kitchen equipment as well as of the occasional exhausted chef, too. The only noticeable change is the patina accrued by serving about two and a half million meals since that first opening day.

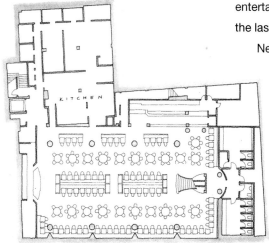

When I first saw the place, it was a huge, dark, damp hole in the ground with a few rats running around. Anything was possible as there was nothing of the original Quag's left except eight enormous columns marching down the length of the room. As our plans progressed, I realized that we had the height to build a

The mezzanine bar.
There is a wonderful
view of the restaurant
from this balcony,
with the mirrors in
the ceiling and along
the walls reflecting
the activity rather
like a kaleidoscope.
The glamorous
marble staircase
leading down to
the restaurant can
cause quite a stir
as girls – and boys –
enjoy making their
entrance. **Below** Plan
of the mezzanine bar.

mezzanine floor that could become a large bar and crustacea counter, reception and coat cupboard (very important!), as well as a marvellous space for a large private room looking down on the spectacle of the restaurant below.

I paid a lot of attention to the art and commissioned eight different artists to paint each of the columns. Christianne Golinelli's ceramic sculptures run along one wall and are reflected in the angled mirrors. Richard Smith's butterflies collect under the mezzanine, and Patrick Cauldfield's jugs punctuate the route to the private room. The front of the crustacea altar is an aquatic mosaic by Biggs and Hunkin. Ned Conran's mural greets you as you come out of the stylish lavatories, and there is a huge Olitski canvas in the private room. My favourite work, though, is Dhura Mistry's bas-relief of a monkey following a woman.

I took an enormous amount of pleasure designing the furniture and accessories for Quag's, and, to my delight, the designs have stood the test of time. The china and glass marked with the simple Q are now classics, and the wine bucket has been used in many of our other restaurants, although with different stands.

Although the French brasseries are the inspiration for Quag's, we wanted to move the food on and make it a bit lighter and fresher. As always, the quality and freshness of the ingredients are the chef's yardsticks. Wonderful, glistening *plateaux de fruits de mer,* with lobsters, langoustines, clams, oysters, crabs and *crevettes grises,* are a constant and popular feature, but also to be savoured are the grilled and rotisseried meats and birds, mounds of *pommes frites*, lightly grilled tuna, classic fish and chips, fresh salads and crisp vegetables, and a slice of excellent terrine of foie gras. The puddings are special, too: pavlova with passion-fruit coulis, sauterne custard with armagnac-soaked prunes, and the finest lemon tart in London.

You can see the energy in the open kitchen, flames jetting off the grill as the marinated meat hits the red-hot metal, the rotisseries loaded with slowly rotating rabbits and birds, and the chef calling out the orders and scrutinising the food as it arrives on the pass. The wine cellar is also very visible, its racks loaded with an enormous supply of bottles ready to be selected and, when appropriate, decanted.

The managers, head waiters and runners, dapper in their Jasper Conran uniforms, work as a well-synchronised team, carrying large trays of food above their heads to the various service stations. Keeping a restaurant of this size working smoothly is a complex logistical exercise, and cooperation between the front-of-house, the kitchen, the washers-up, the wine cellar and the bar is vital, relying not only on excellent staff but on a computerized information and billing system and a manual back-up when it breaks down, which it does from time to time!

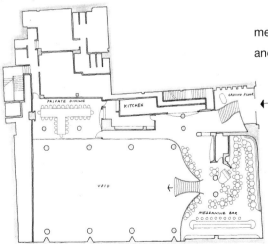

The height of glamour with a real buzz

This page: Above, left to right There's room at Quaglino's for both intimacy and display; Quaglino's modest entrance on Bury Street leads to a shop-cum-reception with menus projected onto the back walls; The main restaurant, with its illuminated skylight that changes as the light changes outside and the spotlit vases of flowers; **Bottom** Stylish details: the excellent lavatories and a cigarette girl.

Opposite page: Top left The aquatic mosaic on the front of the crustacea altar; **Top right** A corner of the restaurant with an angled mirror that reflects the energy of the room; **Bottom left** The curvy staircase from the entrance to the bar; **Bottom right** The private room has a view over the main restaurant has its own dedicated kitchen. It's a very glamorous place to have a party or presentation.

A sense of occasion…

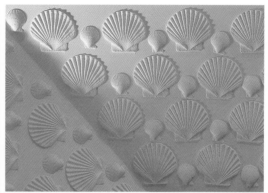

Opposite page, main picture Practically all the fixtures and fittings were specially designed for Quaglino's, but we couldn't resist using these 1930s American aluminium black lacquered prison chairs with coloured silk tassels attached. **Left** Rather sexy bar stools. **Above** Here the Q logo is used in the balustrade for the main staircase. **Top** Plaster bas-relief shells frame the crustacea altar. **Right** Gleaming bronze lobster tails cap the shelf supports of the altar. **Bottom right** Laminated wood and leather bar chairs and zinc-topped tables.

Recipes from Quaglino's

CHEF: Julian O'Neill MANAGER: Kate Grooby

Spicy Beef Salad with Soy and Chilli-pepper Dressing

STARTER Serves 4

dressing:
1 garlic clove, peeled
1 small fresh red chilli
  pepper
1 tbsp light soy
  sauce
1 tbsp lime juice
1 tsp fish sauce
15 g palm sugar

salad:
50 g unsalted fresh
  peanuts
500 g beef fillet
12 cherry tomatoes
½ sweet red pepper
1 small red onion,
  peeled
handful mint leaves
handful coriander
  leaves
vegetable oil

Make the dressing. Finely chop together the garlic and chilli and put in a bowl. Add the rest of the ingredients and mix together until the sugar has dissolved.

Over a low heat in a heavy-based pan, stir the peanuts until they start to colour. Remove and reserve.

Make the salad. Cut the beef into 4 portions and halve the cherry tomatoes. Seed and slice the red pepper and onion. Place all the salad ingredients except the beef in a bowl.

Put a frying pan over a high heat until smoking hot. Add a splash of oil and sear the beef on both sides. The cooking time depends on how you like your beef – 2 minutes each side for rare, 4 minutes for medium to well-done. Remove the beef and rest in a warm place for 10 minutes.

To serve, thinly slice the beef and add it to the salad bowl. Ladle over just enough dressing to coat and toss well.

Sautéd Scallops, with Artichoke and Orange

MAIN Serves 4

4 large globe
  artichokes
5 tbsp extra-virgin
  olive oil
1 medium onion,
  sliced
375 ml dry white
  wine
salt and freshly
  ground black
  pepper

juice of half a lemon
16 scallops
cayenne pepper
3 tbsp butter
3–4 bunches of
  rocket
fresh basil
orange garnish:
2 oranges
4 tbsp sugar
½ tsp vegetable oil

Preheat the oven to 180 °C.

Using a vegetable peeler, peel the oranges and remove all the white pith. Place in a pan with 250 ml water and the sugar, and bring to the boil. Reduce the heat and simmer until the liquid turns syrupy. Remove and drain the peels.

Line a baking sheet with foil and brush with oil. Spread the peels on this so they don't touch. Bake until dry, but not browned – about 15 minutes. Leave to cool. Crumble, then grind to a powder in a spice mill or coffee grinder. Kept in a tightly sealed jar, it will maintain peak flavour for 2 weeks.

Trim the artichokes. Cut off their tops to within 3–4 cm of the base, and remove all but about 1 cm of the stem. Remove all the hard parts from around the artichoke, open up the centre and dig out the choke with a blunt-edged spoon. Trim any remaining hard parts. What is left is the artichoke bottom or fond.

Place 4 tablespoons of oil in a large, deep frying pan over a medium-to-high heat. Add the onion and cook until soft. Lay the artichoke bottoms on the onion and pour over the wine. Bring to the boil, reduce the heat and cover.

Simmer for 30–40 minutes, turning the artichokes occasionally, until tender but not mushy. Remove and reserve 190 ml of the liquid. Cut into bite-sized chunks, and return to the cooking liquid with the remaining oil, salt and pepper, and lemon juice. Keep warm on a very low heat.

Season each scallop with salt and a small sprinkling of cayenne. Place a large non-stick frying pan over a medium-to-high heat and, a minute later, add the butter. Dredge each of the scallops in the orange powder and fry for about 2 minutes on each side until brown.

Divide the rocket between four plates. Top each with a portion of artichokes and 4 scallops. Pour the artichoke liquid over everything and garnish with basil. Sprinkle a little orange powder around the edge of each plate and serve immediately.

Passion-fruit Crème Caramel

DESSERT Serves 4

640 ml whipping
  cream
160 ml milk
8 eggs

160 g sugar
240 g passion-fruit
  purée

Preheat the oven to 120 °C.

In a heavy-based pan, scald the whipping cream and milk. Whisk the eggs and sugar together in a large mixing bowl. Add the purée to the egg mix.

Pour the scalded milk and cream into the purée mix, whisking all the time. Pass through a sieve into individual 120-ml moulds and cook in a bain-marie at 120 °C for 1 hour 20 minutes.

Cool, then refrigerate, turning out of the moulds to serve.

Quaglino's redefined the *fin de siècle* brasserie on a stunning scale. Guests come to enjoy the extraordinary *plateaux de fruits de mer* and an extensive menu of delicious simple dishes.

Above A view over the flannel-grey sofas in the dining room to the servery, where there is a tempting array of hams, sausages, oils, salad, fruit and vegetables. **Opposite page: Left** Plan of the restaurant; **Right** Bar menu: the porcini, fungi and pins and needles link the restaurant to Savile Row.

SARTORIA
bar ristorante

I had longed to open an Italian restaurant in London that was elegant and very simple like the places I remembered from a visit to Milan in the early fifties – plain white cloths on the tables, travertine marble on the floors, and very little else, apart from, of course, the delicious Italian food served by waiters in cream linen jackets. I later discovered that this 1930s style was called Italian Rationalism.

Having acquired a beautifully simple space in 20 Savile Row, I set off to tour northern Italy to remind myself of exactly what it was I loved about this style and how it had stood up to contemporary life. I was very disappointed to find that these simple restaurants had virtually all disappeared; the only place we found remotely in the style was Gatto Nero in Turin. We ended up staying in Mussolini's mistress's house on the shores of Lake Garda, where the food was delicious, but the over-decorated interior anything but rational.

So I started to rifle through my memories of fifty years ago and producing a design for the new restaurant that I believe approximates the simplicity and spirit of the Italian style I so admired, although perhaps with a little more comfort added. Certainly the travertine marble and the white tablecloths have made a comeback. To these I added dark oak panelling, a mid-grey carpet, dark oak chairs with white embroidered antimacassars, flannel-grey upholstered sofas with tan leather bolsters, and a long white marble service counter, with austere white tiles behind. Hams, sausages, and salami hang from a rail behind the bar, and piles of fresh fruit and vegetables sit on the counter. Unusually for a Conran restaurant, the kitchen is out of sight, downstairs in the basement. There are two private rooms, which can be opened with a sliding and folding door to form one large space.

The tailoring trade in Savile Row dictated the restaurant's name, and we have tried to subtly reflect this in the decoration: six bastes (partially made jackets) by six of the most famous tailors of the Row, a collection of paper patterns for Rex Harrison's suits in *My Fair Lady*, and two tailor's dummies. The food reflects the interior – simple and elegant: delicious

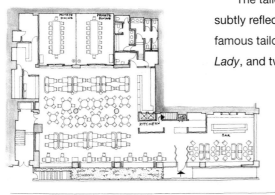

pastas and risottos, excellent Italian sausages and hams, *costaletta milanese*, *tarfutti bianci* in season, the best fish and game, and, of course, outstanding *dolci* and Italian cheeses.

One of the most important attractions of Sartoria is the manager, George Perendes. Endowed with all the good looks and charm of a 1950s Italian film star, he runs the place with wit, ease and efficiency.

Italian rationalism, English tailoring, delectable food and fine wine

Top left Outside Sartoria is a small fragrant garden, which divides the restaurant from the street. A line of windows open out on to a mass of lavender, rosemary, berberis, santolina and box – the perfect surroundings for summer dining. A long glass underlit ramp leads customers from street level to the front door. **Top centre** A view of the bar from the street. Sartoria's bar is a lively place to eat a quick antipasti and drink an *americano* or *negroni* while listening to great piano jazz. **Top right** The main restaurant is very sober – cream walls and ceiling, white linen, pale-grey upholstery,

a travertine floor and brownish grey carpet. Dark oak woodwork holds it all together. **Bottom far left** The staff get a training lecture before beginning service. **Bottom left** One of the private rooms with jacket bastes from famous Savile Row tailors. **Left** Livio Italiano, Sartoria's sommelier, with a bottle from Sartoria's extensive list of over two hundred different Italian wines and grappas. **Bottom left** Sartoria's stylish wine holders. **Right** Sliding dark oak and etched glass doors divide the private rooms from the restaurant – a result of the decision to site the kitchen in the lower floor.

Tailored design and sartorial elegance

Opposite page: Right The tailor's dummy sculptures – *Fat Cow* and *Lardy Boy* – by Jessica Worrall; **Top left** Tailor's shears cutting golden lasagne is Sartoria's trademark. The graphics for the restaurant all reflect the tailoring trade – pins with a porcini mushroom, a tailor's rule and salami, ravioli and pinking shears, a thimble and a bottle of wine; **Bottom left** Patterns for Rex Harrison's Savile Row suits in *My Fair Lady*.

This page: Above, left The bar had to have an espresso machine so we found a beautiful old 1950s model and reconditioned it; **Above, right** Specially designed bar tables add a note of chic; **Right, top to bottom:** Ashtrays, like curled-up tailor's tape measures, are part of Sartoria's graphic scheme; Well-designed bathrooms with ceramic bowl sinks; Fresh mint tea in a beautiful glass pot.

Recipes from Sartoria

CHEF: Piero Boi MANAGER: George Perendes

Carta di Musica with Caprini, Broad Beans, Mint and Basil
STARTER Serves 4

Carta di musica is a crisp unleavened flatbread, a speciality of Sardinia. You can try making it yourself, although it is sold in most good Italian delicatessens. If you don't want to make it and you are unable to buy it, then you can substitute a slice of grilled sourdough bread.

This salad is best made with the first fresh broad beans of the season, before they have formed a coarse skin. If you make this with older beans, they really need to be peeled.

500 g *caprini* (fresh goat's cheese)	2 sheets of *carta di musica*
500 g broad beans, shelled and cooked	juice of half a lemon
bunch of basil	4 tbsp extra-virgin olive oil
bunch of mint	salt and pepper

Crumble the goat's cheese into a bowl and add the broad beans. Coarsely chop the basil and mint and add to the cheese.

Heat the bread under a grill or in the oven.

Dress the goat's cheese mixture with lemon juice and the olive oil, season with salt and pepper and mound on top of the sheets of *carta di musica*, serving immediately so the bread does not go soggy.

Roasted Monkfish with Salsicia Piccante, Clams and Cannellini Beans
MAIN Serves 4

If you are unable to get clams, you can happily substitute mussels.

800-g to 1-kg monkfish fillet	24 carpet shell clams
200 g spicy Italian sausage	400 g cooked cannellini beans
2 garlic cloves, peeled and finely chopped	2 tbsp flat-leaf parsley, chopped
	100 ml fish or vegetable stock

Cut monkfish into 3-cm pieces and the sausage into 1-cm slices.

Place a heavy-based frying pan over a medium-to-high heat until smoking hot. Cut the monkfish into 3-cm pieces and seal briefly on both sides before adding the sausage. Stir, then add the garlic, clams, cannellini beans and parsley. Add the stock, shake pan and wait for the clams to open. Let the liquid reduce slightly, and serve immediately in soup plates garnished with a little more parsley.

Zabaglione
DESSERT Serves 4

Zabaglione is one of the best-known Italian desserts, a warm frothy custard flavoured with Marsala sweet wine.

8 egg yolks	4 Italian sponge fingers
200 g caster sugar	
100 ml Marsala	

Put on a pan of water and bring to the boil. In a bowl that will sit over the water and using an electric whisk, beat the yolks and sugar until pale and frothy and doubled in volume. Put over the water and continue whisking until you have a smooth custard. Whisk in the Marsala, a splash at a time, tasting as you go until you have a well-balanced flavour. If it shows signs of turning to scrambled egg, quickly pour in more wine.

Pour into suitable glasses to serve, putting a sponge finger next to each.

Regional Italian cooking in an elegant Savile Row dining-room draws a fashionable and discerning clientele seven days a week. The entirely Italian wine list is unique in London.

Above A view down the Heddon Street Zinc towards the kitchen and over the marble-topped tables. Good solid furnishings for the rough-and-tumble of everyday British life. **Opposite page: Left** Plan of the Heddon Street Zinc; **Right** Honest house wine with its own Zinc label.

ZINC
BAR • GRILL

As you might expect, Zinc was inspired by those wonderful cafés that were once a feature of every French market town – a place where you could always drop in for a *café au lait*, a *bière pression* or a simple meal with a carafe of wine. There was an easy democratic buzz about the place, a strong smell of sweat and Gitanes, and a lot of Gallic good humour. Sadly, they now seem to have disappeared and replaced with fast-food joints. I thought I'd try to find a way of reviving them in Britain and, in the process, find a way of stemming the American fast-food invasion and speed up the demise of those dreary themed pubs.

So Zinc, which first opened in Heddon Street, off Regent Street, at the end of 1997, is our attempt to find a formula that can expand in towns and cities throughout the UK – and who knows where else? So far, we have opened branches in Manchester, Birmingham and Edinburgh, with other sites planned in London and elsewhere.

The basic formula is simple. Large zinc bars serve a wide selection of wines, champagne, spirits, cocktails and, of course, beer. Good, inexpensive grills and comfortable food is prepared and cooked in kitchens that are an integral part of the space and clearly visible. Straightforward, durable furnishings feature leather banquettes, bentwood chairs, wooden or marble tables, and wooden or stone floors. There are sturdy plates and cutlery, bold graphics and paper menus. Everything is simple and cheerful and very reasonably priced. Rather than following a cookie-cutter formula, though, every Zinc is designed to be appropriate to its locality. No two Zincs will ever be identical in appearance, even if the philosophy behind them remains constant.

We always look for sites where there is an outdoor/indoor aspect because sitting outside having a coffee or a beer is a great and often unrealized British dream. Heddon Street was the perfect site, with a large pavement running the whole width of the property and a pedestrianised cobbled street in front. Inside is a large space, with skylights at the back and the original cast-iron columns spanning the room. The columns act as a perfect place to hang coats, adding to the air of breezy informality.

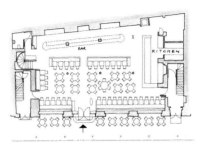

In Heddon Street we have decorated the walls with Tessa Trager's remarkable photographs of peasants' hands holding vegetables dug straight from the soil. In Manchester there are late-19th-century French graphics advertising pâtisserie, *charcuteries*, *boucheries* and *boulangeries*. Zincs in Edinburgh and Birmingham will be different again. Bar music plays an important role in the evening entertainment and adds to the buzz. Wherever they are, Zincs are intended as cheerful, enjoyable places with good food and lots of drink.

Think Zinc: a revolution in the making?

Clockwise from top left (all at Heddon Street):
Red laminate tables in front of the banquettes, with a view across the restaurant to the front door; The etched glass screen helps to divide the bar from the restaurant; Outdoor seating for a cup of coffee or a beer is a vital component of all the Zinc bars and grills; The buzz of a busy Zinc; The large private room adjoins cellars filled with stacked wine bottles; The zinc-topped bar is at the back of the restaurant and is a very important part of the Zinc mix.

Design classics: bold, simple and cheerful

Opposite page The stylish zinc Zinc ashtray, big enough not to be easily stolen – note the bold Zinc graphics on the matchbox. **This page: Above, left to right** The furniture is designed to be durable – Zincs have to survive the wear and tear inflicted by the sometimes raucous great British public; Menu holder and sign outside; Cocktails are an important part of the Zinc mix; **Right** Copper rivets fix the zinc front to the bar.

Recipes from Heddon Street Zinc

CHEF: Paul Jewson MANAGER: Nicola Williams

Spinach and Goat's Cheese Tart

STARTER Makes 10 portions

25.5-cm shortcrust tart shell, baked blind
1.5 kg picked and washed spinach
500 g fresh goat's cheese, broken into small pieces
100 g Reggiano Parmigiano, grated
125 g cream cheese
2 eggs
2 egg yolks
125 ml double cream

salt and coarsely ground pepper
tapenade:
120 g pitted black olives
60 g anchovy fillets
60 g capers
100 ml extra-virgin olive oil
black pepper
to serve:
150 g rocket leaves
balsamic vinegar
extra-virgin olive oil

In a large pot of boiling salted water, blanch the spinach for a few seconds to wilt, and refresh instantly in iced water. Drain and set aside.

Put the cream cheese, eggs, egg yolks and double cream in a food processor. Season with a good pinch of coarsely cracked black pepper and blend until smooth.

Preheat the oven to 170 °C.

Place half the cheese evenly around the base of the tart case. Distribute the spinach around the tart, allowing it to sit up in ribbons. Place the remaining cheese over the spinach. Carefully spoon the blended ingredients over the tart to filling point. Bake for 30–35 minutes or until just set.

Blitz the tapenade ingredients in a food processor to a rough paste.

Serve the tart warm with a turned dessert spoon of tapenade and sprigs of rocket dressed with balsamic vinegar and olive oil on each plate.

Spiced Mussels with Lemongrass, Coconut Milk and Chilli

MAIN Serves 4

South-east Asian favours offer a different take on mussel soup.

300 ml tamarind water
½ bunch Thai basil
½ bunch mint
½ bunch coriander
2.5-cm cube galangal
roots from 1 bunch coriander
2 small green chillies
1 tsp fish sauce
1 tsp palm sugar
50 ml lime juice

1 stalk lemongrass
300 ml coconut milk
nam jim (chilli jam), to taste
2 kg cleaned mussels
garnish:
4 lime leaves, shredded
4 hot red chillies, shredded
2 limes

Bruise all the aromatic ingredients in a pestle with a mortar. Transfer to a bowl and wash the pestle and mortar. Put the fish sauce and palm sugar in the mortar and work to a paste. When smooth, add the lime juice and incorporate. Return the aromatics to the mortar and work altogether until you have a smooth and coherent sauce.

Cut the lemongrass into 7-cm-long batons and bruise. Put them in a large pan with the coconut milk and bring slowly to the boil, then add 2 tsp chilli jam and stir in. Taste, adding more chilli jam if it is not hot enough for your liking.

Add the mussels, cover and steam until they open – about 3–4 minutes.

To serve, ladle into large warmed bowls and top with some herbs, lime leaf and chilli. Garnish with a halved lime.

Fresh Fruit with Tequila and Lime Sorbet

DESSERT Serves 6

500 ml caster sugar
finely grated rind of 4 limes
2 tbsp tequila
juice of 12 limes
¼ pineapple

8 strawberries
3 white peaches
15 raspberries
1 punnet redcurrants
1 banana leaf

Make a sugar syrup. In a heavy-based saucepan, bring the sugar to the boil with 500 ml of water. Reduce the heat until just the occasional bubble breaks the surface. Add the lemon rinds and simmer for 10 minutes. Remove from the heat, cool to room temperature, pass through a sieve and refrigerate until needed.

Mix together the tequila, lime juice and syrup and churn until set in an ice-cream maker or set into a shallow tray in the freezer overnight.

Wash the banana leaf and cut into 10-cm squares. Peel and cut the pineapple into eighths lengthways. Hull and halve the strawberries.

Put a square of banana leaf on each plate, putting a scoop of the sorbet on top and garnish with the fresh fruits.

A busy brasserie just off Regent Street, this Zinc offers an eclectic menu that includes many favourite dishes from around the world.

Index

Address Book

Alcazar
62 rue Mazarine
75006 Paris, France
+33 (0) 1 53 10 19 99

Bibendum
Michelin House, 81 Fulham Road
London SW3 6RD
020 7581 5817

Blue Print Café
28 Shad Thames
London SE1 2YD
020 7378 7031

Bluebird
350 King's Road
London SW3 5UU
020 7559 1000 (Restaurant)
020 7559 1153 (Foodstore)
020 7559 1129 (Club)

Butlers Wharf Chop House
The Butlers Wharf Building
36e Shad Thames
London SE1 2YE
020 7403 3403

Cantina del Ponte
The Butlers Wharf Building
36c Shad Thames
London SE1 2YE
020 7403 5403

Coq d'Argent
No.1 Poultry
London EC2R 8EJ
020 7395 5000

Great Eastern Hotel:
Aurora
Liverpool Street
London EC2M 7QN
020 7618 7000

Fishmarket
Bishopsgate
London EC2M 7QN
020 7618 7200

George
Liverpool Street
London EC2M 7QN
020 7618 7300

Miyabi
Liverpool Street
London EC2M 7QN
020 7618 7100

Terminus
Liverpool Street
London EC2M 7QN
020 7618 7400

Guastavino's
409 East 59th Street
between First and York Avenue
New York NY 10022
+1 212 980 2455

Mezzo
100 Wardour Street
London W1F 0TN
020 7314 4000

Orrery
55 Marylebone High Street
London W1M 3AE
020 7616 8000

Le Pont de la Tour
The Butlers Wharf Building
36d Shad Thames
London SE1 2YE
020 7403 8403 (Restaurant, Bar & Grill)
020 7403 4030 (Foodstore)
020 7403 2403 (The Wine Merchant)
020 7234 3664 (Coffee Kiosk)

Quaglino's
16 Bury Street
London SW1Y 6AJ
020 7930 6767

Sartoria
20 Savile Row
London W1X 1AE
020 7534 7000

Zinc Bar & Grill (London)
21 Heddon Street
London W1R 7LF
020 7255 8899

Zinc Bar & Grill (Manchester)
The Triangle
Hanging Ditch
Manchester M4 3ES
0870 333 4333

Zinc Bar & Grill (Birmingham)
The Pavilion, Regency Wharf, Broad Street,
Birmingham
0870 333 4333

Zinc Bar & Grill (Edinburgh)
Ocean Terminal
Ocean Drive, Leith
Edinburgh EH6 7DZ
0870 333 4333

Ocean Kitchen
Ocean Terminal
Ocean Drive, Leith
Edinburgh EH6 7DZ
0870 333 4333

Berns
(designed and managed by Conran)
Berzelii Park
PO Box 16340
SE 103 27
Stockholm, Sweden
+46 (0) 8 566 322 22

Acknowledgements

This book is dedicated to the whole team of directors, managers, chefs, and particularly the washers up, kitchen staff, waiters and waitresses, bar staff, buyers, artists, contractors, even lawyers and planners (on occasions). Also to my colleagues, the architects and designers from Conran & Partners who have worked so hard with me over the years to make our restaurants, bars, clubs, cafés and delis such a success.

There are also many builders, shop-fitting contractors, electricians, kitchen suppliers, artists and technicians to thank who have made a significant contribution to the fitting out of our restaurants. I would particularly like to praise all the people at Benchmark who have made so much of the furniture and fittings so very well, very often at very short notice – thank you.

My thanks to Sam Newman who has typed, retyped and typed again, and to Vicki who has read, corrected and recorrected.

The chefs and managers listed are correct at the time of printing, but are always liable to change in the future.

First published in 2001 by
Conran Octopus Limited
a part of Octopus Publishing Group
2–4 Heron Quays
London E14 4JP

www.conran-octopus.co.uk

Text copyright © Terence Conran 2001
Photographs copyright © Conran Ink Limited 2001
Plans of the restaurants copyright © Conran & Partners 2001
Design and layout copyright © Conran Octopus 2001

Publishing Director: Lorraine Dickey
Senior Editor: Muna Reyal
Recipe editor: Richard Whittington
Copyeditor: Robert Anderson

Creative Director: Leslie Harrington
Designers: Lisa Sheard and Carl Hodson
Photography: Georgia Glynn Smith
Plans of the restaurants: Hing Chan

Production Director: Zoe Fawcett

British Library Cataloguing-in-Publication Data. A catalogue record for this book is available from the British Library.

ISBN 1 84091 234 0

Colour origination by Sang Choy International, Singapore

Printed in China